THE MATHERS
ON DANCING

The Mathers on Dancing

By JOSEPH E. MARKS III

Including An Arrow Against Profane and Promiscuous Dancing Drawn out of the Quiver of the Scriptures, *by Increase Mather* (1685)

Also A Cloud of Witnesses, *by Cotton Mather* (c. 1700)

With A Bibliography of Anti-Dance Books (1685-1963)

Published by Dance Horizons, 1801 *East* 26th Street, Brooklyn, N.Y. 11229

International Standard Book Number 0-87127-063-3
Library of Congress Catalog Card Number 75-9156

Printed in the United States of America

FOR

MY

MOTHER

❧ ❧ ❧ ❧ ❧ ❧ ❧ ❧ ❧ ❧ ❧ ❧ ❧ ❧ ❧ ❧ ❧ ❧

Table of
CONTENTS.

THE MATHERS

ON DANCING

IN BOSTON, at the corner of Prison Lane, next to the Town house, the Dutch Bookseller, Joseph Brunning, displayed a small, thirty-page tract. It had been printed February 16, 1685-6 (i.e. 1685), by Samuel Green and carried the lengthy title, *An Arrow Against Profane and Promiscuous Dancing Drawn out of the Quiver of the Scriptures*. Although the title page showed it was written by the "Ministers of Christ at Boston," most people knew that its author was Increase Mather. Mather, in this case as in many others, was acting as spokesman for the ministers.

Increase Mather, the son of the famous Puritan divine Richard Mather and the son-in-law of the even more famous Puritan John Cotton, was born in Dorchester, Massachusetts, June 21, 1639. After finishing his A.B. degree at Harvard and his M.S. degree at Trinity College, Dublin, Ireland, he went to England where he gained a pastorate. He would like to have stayed, but his conservative Puritan conscience began to bother him when he found he could not accept Anglicanism. He returned home and to his father's church.

In 1681, the Second Church in Boston elected him as its minister. With such an important appointment he became an influential leader in both civic and church affairs. John Dunton, the English bookseller, writes of a visit to Mather in these words, "So I made my first visit to that Reverend and Learned Divine, Mr. Increase Mather. He's the Present Rector of Harvard College: He is deservedly called, The Metropolitan Clergy-Man of the Kingdom."[1] One of his former enemies, Benjamin Colman, said after Mather's death on August 23, 1723, "He was the patriarch and prophet among us, if even one might be so called."[2]

In 1684, Charles II of England annulled the Charter of Massachusetts. Four years later the people of New England called upon Mather to speak for the colony. He went to England; and, while he was unable to restore the old charter, Mather did get a new one that allowed him to appoint all the officers reserved to the crown.

This incident, like the King Philip's War, was one more sign to Mather that the Lord was displeased with Boston. The good Puritan could not sit idly by and watch Boston slip slowly away from the Lord and the teaching of the first generation. He felt compelled to do everything he could to bring Boston back to the Lord. At every sign of degeneration Mather saw, he would preach a sermon or write a tract about it. The

1. John Dunton, John Dunton's Letters from New England (Boston, 1867). Letter III to Mr. George Larkin dated: Boston in New England, March 25, 1686. p. 74.

2. Quoted in Allen Johnson and Dumas Malone, eds., Dictionary of American Biography (New York, 1928-44), XII, p. 393.

minister knew it was his duty, and if he shirked it, he would lose his own soul. Increase Mather had made a covenant with the Lord.

Just as the band of people who set sail on the *Arebella* in 1629 had bound themselves with a covenant, so Mather bound himself by the same covenant. John Winthrop had stated plainly the reasons and conditions of the covenant in his sermon aboard ship when he said:

Thus stands the cause between God and us: we are entered into covenant with Him for this work; we have taken out a commission, the Lord hath given us leave to draw our own articles. We have professed to enterprise these actions upon these and these ends; we have hereupon besought Him of favor and blessing. Now if the Lord shall please to hear us and bring us in peace to the place we desire, then hath He ratified this covenant and sealed our Commission, [and] will expect a strict performance of the articles contained in it. But if we shall neglect the observation of these articles which are the ends we have propounded, and dissembling with our God, shall fail to embrace this world and prosecute our carnal intentions, seeking great things for ourselves and our posterity, the Lord will surely break out in wrath against us, be revenged of such perjured people, and make us know the price of the breach of such a covenant.[3]

3. *John Winthrop,* A Model of Christian Charity, *in* The American Puritans, *ed. Perry Miller (Garden City, 1956), p. 83.*

Because God had caused the first generation to arrive safely and had helped them prosper, they felt He was pleased: that their "city upon the hill," as John Winthrop had called it, would have "the eyes of all the people" upon it; that Boston and New England could now show the world what God had intended when He started the Reformation.[4]

4. For a greater discussion of the Puritan mind and thought see Perry Miller's interesting and penetrating studies: The New England Mind. The 17th Century (Cambridge, Mass., 1939) and From Colony to Province (Cambridge, Mass., 1953). For a discussion of declension in New England see Perry Miller's, "Declension in a Bible Commonwealth," Proceedings, American Antiquarian Society, N.S. 51(1941), pp. 27-94.

Some forty years later Increase Mather watched with fearfulness as he saw Boston and New England grow from hamlet to town, colony to province. As he watched the immigrants arrive, many of whom had not joined into the covenant between man and God, he feared for the "Bible Commonwealth." Mather watched them as they introduced the worldly sins from the old country to the second and third generation New Englander, who had already shown signs of backsliding.

As God had given His signs of displeasure by plagues, wars, fires, and other mishaps, Mather and the other ministers had seen the signs and believed it was their duty to bring the unregenerated into line, lest God should break his treaty and all would fall.

Many of the people of Boston, however, were less concerned, as they went about embracing the "present world" and prosecuting their "carnal intentions." Dunton, writing about Boston a year after the *Arrow* was written, states: "Their Laws for Reformation of Manners, are very severe yet but little regarded by the People, so at least to make 'em better, or cause 'em to mend their manners."[5]

5. *Dunton, p.* 71

Cotton Mather, son of Increase Mather, writes in his *Magnalia Christi Americana* that the:

people began more notoriously to forget the *errand into the wilderness*, and when the enchantments of *this world* caused the rising generation more sensibly to neglect the primitive designs and interest of religion propounded by their fathers; a *change* in the tenour of the devine dispensation toward this country, was quickly the matter of everybody's observations.[6]

6. *Hartford,* 1820, *II,* p. 270.

The General Court had tried to bring about a reformation of the evils that plagued the city. They had ordered a synod to convene in Boston on September 10, 1679, to find "what are the evils that have provoked the Lord to bring his Judgement on New England?" and "What is to be done, that so these evils may be reformed?"

Increase Mather, in writing the report for Court and the ministers, found the "Lord's controversie with the people of New England" as a decay of Godliness among many professors in the church, pride in respect of apparel, contention and the breaking of the second commandment. He also found that "the name of God had been polluted and profaned," that there was much Sabbath-breaking and intemperance. For the last sin mentioned he says:

And there are other hainous breaches of the seventh commandment. Temptations thereunto are become too common, *viz.* such as immodest apparel, *Prov.* 7:10 laying out of hair, borders, naked necks and arms, or which is more abominable naked breast and mixed dancings, light behaviour, and expressions,. . . ."[7]

7. *The tract that Increase Mather wrote was called:* The Necessity of Reformation, *and is quoted in Cotton Mather's* Magnalia, II, 274-282. *My quotes are from this copy. See also,* Thomas J. Holmes, Increase Mather, A Bibliography of His Works, *(Cleveland, 1931),* II, p. 369.

Just as we cite a decay in family government as a cause for today's evils, so Mather found that "Most of the evils that abound amongst us, proceed from defects as to family government." To correct these evils Mather concluded that all the people should strengthen the covenant and walk closer to God, that days of fasting and humiliation should be set aside, and that the laws should be strengthened and carried out. And by such actions they would regain God's grace and the religious fever as was known by the first generation.

Because people are people the advice of the court and ministers was carried out and followed for a short time, but soon they fell to their "sins" once again. Boston was no longer a community of a few hundred souls but had grown to be the largest town in America, at the time. In 1685, with an estimated census of 7,000 inhabitants, it was able to support not only the necessities of its people but many of the luxuries. With the wealth came artisan shops, bookstores, imported clothes and dancing masters. As a seaport town, it developed a successful shipbuilding industry and a thriving trade with other countries.

Mather and the ministers saw that with economic expansion and wealth came a waning of public morals, as the people began turning their attention from religion to commerce. Therefore, they began to preach about little else than the sins of man and the loss of religion as practiced by their fathers. It is through these sermons that we are able to reconstruct in some measure the life of Boston during the period. It was such a sermon that Increase Mather wrote when he penned *An Arrow Against Profane and Promiscuous Dancing.*

The Puritans were not against all forms of dancing. Percy A. Scholes in his book, *The Puritans and Music in England and New England,*[8] has taken great pains to set the matter straight. They were, however, against dancing when it was associated with feast or public demonstrations. Where danc-

8. *London, 1934.*

ing was justified by the Bible, it was not wrong, so long as it was used as the Bible stated it should be used.

Even mixed dancing was not condemned by John Cotton, although many Puritans did condemn it. Cotton could justify it by the Bible. In answer to the question about mixed dancing he wrote R. Levett of Boston, England, on March 3, 1625:

Dancing (yea though mixt) I would not simply condem. For I see two sorts of mixt dancings in use with God's people in the Old Testament, the one religious, Exod. XV, 20,21, and other civil, tending to the prase of conquerors, as the former of God, I Sam. XVII, 6,7. Only lascivious dancing to wanton ditties, and amorous gestures and wanton dalliances, especially after feasts, I would bear witness against, as a great *flabella libidinis*.[9]

9. Quoted in Joseph E. Marks III, America Learns to Dance (New York, 1957), p. 15.

Increase Mather and the ministers of Boston make it plain in the first paragraph of the *Arrow* that they are not against all dancing. To make sure there is no misunderstanding they state about halfway through the tract, "Understand him [Plutarch] and the other authors cited, as speaking of Promiscuous *Dances*."[10]

10. Increase Mather, Arrow, p. 45.

Mixed, gynaecandrical, impleaded, petulant, profane and promiscuous dancing were all under the same category. All, according to the ministers, caused sexual excitement and therefore sinned against the Seventh Commandment: "Thou shalt not commit adultery." However, where dance was used to teach manners, and according to Puritan thought manners were a part of morals, they could justify its use. But make no mistake, each sex must be taught by itself.

The ministers of New England had had trouble with dancing from the beginning. In 1628 when Morton set up his Maypole at Merry Mount and began "drinking and dancing aboute it . . . like so many fairies, or furies rather," and then composing "sundry rimes & verses, some tending to licenciousnes," which were sung as they danced, John Endecott and his friend John Bradford felt it was too close to the pagan feast "of ye Roman Goddess Flora"; Endecott ordered the Maypole cut down and "rebuked them for their profannes."[11]

Even though the Puritan ministers disliked the use of the Maypole and its pagan rites, the use of the Maypole continued for some time. Although the ministers had published their views about dance in the *Arrow*, Judge Samuel Sewall was able to write on May 26, 1687, that the people of Charlestown had cut down one Maypole and that "Now a bigger is set up and a garland upon

11. *William Bradford, Bradford's History of 'Plimoth Plantation,' (Boston, 1898), pp285-288. See also; Charles Francis Adams, Three Episodes of Massachusetts History (Boston, 1892), I, ch. 2.*

{ 9 }

it." The next day he wrote that he had "overheard some discourse about the Maypole, and told what manner it was in England to dance about it with music; and that 'twas to be feared such practices would be here."[12]

12. Quoted in Marks, p. 16.

Increase Mather writes in *A Testimony Against several Prophane and Superstitious Customes* . . .about *"the Talk which passeth amongst some Vain Persons, concerning a Maypole which they intend to set up when the Time shall come."* While he sees such actions as a sign of degeneration, he seems less worried about the dancing than the giving of "Honour to that great Whore" Flora.[13]

13. *Holmes,* Increase Mather, *II, p.* 569.

The number of court cases and laws forbidding dance attest the fact that there was dancing throughout this early period. In Cambridge, in 1638, Lawrence Waters' wife and friend were brought to court, and they "were admonished to avoyed dancing." In the town of Duxburrow, Samuel Eaton and his wife Halle were "released with admonition" for mixed dancing. Also, in the same year the court "observed that there were many abuses & disorders by dancinge in ordinaryes, wheather mixt or unmixt, upon marriage or some p[er]son" and thereby passed a law stating dancing would not be allowed in ordinaries. The law does not say that all dancing was forbidden, only tavern dancing; but where it was used in the right place and at the right time it was allowed. Most of the people who were brought to court for dancing were charged with some other offence also.[14]

Mather's comments in the *Arrow* to the plea that "Such dancing is now become customary amongst Christians" indicates that dance was a popular form of amusement, although he admonishes the good Christians to "swim against the stream" and to "Keep themselves pure from the sins of the Times of which this of mixed dancing is none of the lease."[15] A year later he wrote in the preface of *A Testimony Against Several Prophane and Superstitious Customes*, that "last Year Promiscuous Dancing was *openly practiced, and too much countenanced in this Degenerated Town.*"[16] That was the same year he had written the *Arrow*.

If people are going to dance, then it will not be long before a dancing master will be around to instruct them in the latest dances. The Puritans had countenanced the Puritan publication of John Playford's *The English Dancing Master* with its rules to country dancing.[17] As the ships brought new people to the Boston shores, they brought with them the latest dances from their homeland. The people of Boston no doubt found the

14. *Quoted in Marks, p.* 16.

15. *Increase Mather, Arrow, p.* 53.

16. *Holmes,* Increase Mather, *II, p.* 569.

17. *Marks, pp.* 18, 22.

{ *11* }

Jigs and Galliards that Mather speaks of in the *Arrow* a welcome change from the country dances.[18] But Jigs and Galliards call for dancing masters.

18. *Increase Mather,* Arrow, p. 48.

Mather in speaking of Jigs and Galliards no doubt was also interested in the lively nature of both dances. For while the Jig was popular at the time and has continued to be popular to our own day, the Galliard was more popular during the time of Queen Elizabeth I. Melusine Wood speaking of the Galliard says, "The emphasis was on energy and agility rather than subtlety and restraint, and following these lines the Galliard eventually ceased to be a dance and became an acrobatic display." But by the last half of the seventeenth century the Galliard had been altered to become a less active dance and was soon forgotten.[19] The dances that were in use during the period were the Minuet, Bourree, Passepied, Rigaudon, Loure, as well as the country dances.

19. *Melusine Wood,* Some Historical Dances *(London, 1952), pp. 93,* 119.

Unfortunately for dance, the first dancing masters who came to Boston were not of the highest character and brought the wrath of the Boston ministers down upon their heads. In 1676, "one dancing school was set up, but put down." Then, in 1681, according to the *Records of the Court of Assistants,* a Frenchman, named Henry Sherlot, tried to set up a school; but, as he was a "person very Insolent & of ill fame that Rause & scoffes at Religion, of a Turbulent spirit no way fitt to be tolerated to live in this place . . .," he was ordered not only out of town but out of the colony.[20]

20. *Quoted in Marks, p. 19.*

After Sherlot came the famous Francis Stepney, who by his bold statements caused the ministers to convene and state their case against mixed dancing. It is in the tract *An Arrow against Profane and Promiscuous Dancing Drawn out of the Quiver of the Scriptures* that we learn how the ministers felt about mixed dancing. As to the Stepney incident, Judge Sewall wrote in his diary for November 12, 1685:

After, the Ministers of this Town came to court and complained against a Dancing Master who seeks to set up here and hath mixt Dances, and his time of Meeting is Lecture-Day; and 'tis reported he should say that by one Play he could teach more Divinity than Mr. Willard or the Old Testament. Mr. Moody said 'Twas not time for N.E. to dance. Mr. Mather struct at the Root, speaking against mixt Dances.[21]

21. *Ibid.*

The court ordered Stepney not to keep a dancing school: "if he does will be taken in contempt and be proceeded with accordingly." Stepney was fined 100 pounds for his "Blasphemous words and Reviling the Government," and he showed an even greater lack of character when he ran away from

22. Ibid. his debt.[22]

The ministers were not alone in their feelings about Stepney; when he tried to enter New York in 1687, the governor's council forbade him to teach and ordered him out of the province, unless he were able to show that he would not become a public charge. Stepney, feeling he was unjustly accused, sent a petition to the council which granted him permission to appeal to the king in person. Whether the permission was granted or 23. Ibid., p. 22. not is not known.[23]

As we read through the *Arrow* it is not difficult to find the allusions to Stepney and his bold statements. In Mather's answer to Plea 2 that *"The Design of Dancing is only to teach Children good Behaviour and decent Carriage,"* he states: "If therefore any be disposed to have their children instructed in that which may be truely ornamental, or a desirable Accomplishment in these respect they may send them not to a Blasphemer, but some Grave Person that will teach them Decency of Behaviour, not Promiscuously, but each sex by themselves; 24. *Increase Mather, Arrow, p. 52.* so neither God nor Man will be offended."[24]

In Plea 3 he pointed another arrow at Stepney when he wrote, "If a Blasphemer shall tell them, There's as good Divinity to be learned by a Play as by the Scripture itself, perhaps they may be debauched into belief of it."[25] He again strikes at the dancing master with "Not that Dancing, or Music, or Singing are in themselves sinful: but if the Dancing Master be wicked they are commonly abused to lasciviousness, and that makes them become abominable."[26] The ministers succeeded in getting rid of Stepney, as they had done those that had preceded him. Had Stepney and the other dance teachers of which we have a record conducted themselves with the manners and morals that the Puritans felt should be gained from dance, they no doubt would have been allowed to stay, but under the ever present and watchful eye of the ministers.

Though the ministers stated their views in the *Arrow* and succeeded in ridding Boston of undesirable dance teachers, it was not long before the dance teachers were back. Cotton Mather, as always, following in the footsteps of his father and grandfather, had his controversy with dance.

Cotton Mather, the last of the great Mather dynasty, was born February 12, 1663. To him fell the lot of a Puritanism that was fast fading away. Being born into a family of Puritan ministers he began to see him-

25. *Ibid., p.* 53.

26. *Ibid., p.* 58

self appointed by birth as the one to carry on the Congregational ideals of his father and grandfathers.

He entered Harvard at eleven years of age, being the youngest student ever to enter the institution. He was not liked by his fellow students, some of whom considered him a prig. His correcting of the less pious ones was often returned by hazing. He carried the same attitude throughout life and often received the same actions in return. He was a controversial figure, though a great influence on the thinking of his time. He longed to be influential in the political field, but his frequent arrogance and aggressiveness, plus his hot temper, did little to enhance his position along this line. While he lost popularity in many fields he always remained a leader in the church. Cotton Mather received a call from the Second Church, where he worked closely with his father, taking the elder Mather's position after his death.

Dunton in writing of a visit to Cotton Mather says:

And next to him [Increase] in Fame, (whom I likewise visited at the same time) is his son Mr. Cotton Mather, an Excellent Preacher, a great Writer; He has very lately finish'd the Church History of New England, which I'm going to print; And which is more than all, He Lives the

Doctrine he Preaches. . . . . As to the Discorse that past between us, 'tis not proper to insert here; but I must say, I am greatly wanting to myself, if I did not learn more in an hour I enjoy'd his Company, than I cou'd in an Age spent in other Mens."[27]

27. *Dunton, p.* 75.

Cotton Mather's controversy was not so much with the dance teachers as with balls and dancing parties. His tract written in 1700[?] was entitled: *A Cloud of Witnessess; Darting out Light upon a CASE, too Unseasonably made Seasonable to be Discoursed on.* In the first paragraph he let it be known to all that he did not approve of balls and mixed dancing. Like his father, he did not find it wrong for parents to send their children to a dancing master where they might learn to carry themselves handsomely in company. The question that worried Cotton Mather was whether balls, which "Lead the Young People of both Sexes unto great Liberties with each other," are not a "Vanity which is forbidden by Christianity."[28]

28. *Cotton Mather, Cloud, p.* 65.

Mather's *Cloud of Witnesses* gives some clue that there were dancing masters in and around Boston at the turn of the century even though we do not read of another one until 1712. At that time George Brownell, whom Benjamin Franklin writes of as having been his teacher, opened a school where he not only taught music, but "Writing,

Cyphering, Dancing" and needlework. Four years later he advertised that he taught "Dancing cheaper than ever was taught in Boston."[29]

29. *Marks, p.* 30.

Mather, in his funeral sermon for the famous school master Exekiel Cheever, who had been principal of the Boston Latin School until his death in 1708; gives another clue that there were dance teachers in Boston at that time. Mather said: "I can't but observe with just indignation; to *Feed* our Children, to Cloth our Children, to do anything for the Bodies of our Children; or perhaps *to teach some trifle at a* Dancing School, scarcely worth their learning, we account no expense too much."[30]

30. *Quoted in Scholes, p.* 65.

Mather does not condemn the dancing master provided he teaches each sex by itself and he is of good character. But Mather does gather his witness against those nonconformist ministers who spoke out for balls and mixed dancing. One such minister could have been Timothy Edwards, father of Jonathan Edwards, who after an ordination, had a dance at his house at Windsor Farmes, Connecticut, in 1694.[31]

31. *Henry Bamford Parke,* Jonathan Edwards, the Fiery Puritan *(New York,* 1930), *p.* 4.

Increase Mather gives one of the main reasons (and no doubt Cotton Mather for the same reason) for his composing the tract against mixed dancing when he writes at the end of the *Arrow:*

What will you say in the day of the Lords pleading with you? We have that charity for you as to
believe that you have erred through Ignorance,
and now wickedly: and we have therefore accounted it our Duty to inform you in the Truth.
If you resolve not on Reformation, you will be
left inexcusable. However it shall be, we have
now given our testimony and delivered our own
Souls. *Consider what we say, and the Lord will
give you understanding in all things.*[32]

32. *Increase Mather,
Arrow,* p. 59.

Let us remember that Mather was a true
believer of the communal covenant and that
it was his duty as minister to warn the people that, if they broke the covenant, God
would show His wrath and all would fall.
However, by his showing the people where
they had erred, he would be performing his
duty to God, and at least save his own soul.

Both Increase Mather's *Arrow* and Cotton
Mather's *Cloud of Witnesses* have been
used over and over again by the historian
and those writers who desired to show what
dance was like during the Puritan period. In
most cases selections were drawn out of
context and therefore painted the gloomy
and dour picture that we have so long had
about our Puritan forefathers. The great
value of both tracts is that they are the first
and only tracts that have come to light so far
that give a clear picture of what the ministers thought about dance. It was not until

Percy Scholes exploded the "gloomy theory" about the Puritan ideas on music and dance, that the historian has changed his thought and writings about them. While Scholes explores the *Arrow* with much care and Perry Miller and Thomas H. Johnson in *The Puritans* gives a long excerpt, it has not been printed in full.[33] Only by reading both tracts in full can a really true picture be obtained.

33. *New York*, 1938, pp. 411-413.

From a literary point of view, both the *Arrow* and the *Cloud of Witnesses* are what Perry Miller has described as the jeremiad.[34] The jeremiad was the literary type that was developed by the first native-born Americans. While the jeremiad was a fast day sermon, it carried a certain formula. This form of sermon exhorted the people to remember the covenant and the ways of the founding fathers. Filled with texts mainly from Isaiah or Jeremiah, the jeremiad lamentated New England's present fall from Grace. As Miller states:

34. *Miller*, Colony, ch. II.

But the real substance of the discourse came at the end, in the "application" or "uses," where the preacher spelled out the significance of the situation. Here he enumerated, in as much detail as he had courage for, the provocations to vengeance, proposed a scheme or reformation, and let his imagination glow over still more exquisite judgments yet in store unless his listeners acted upon his recommendations.[35]

35. *Ibid. p.* 29.

Increase Mather follows that group of Puritans who wrote in the "Plain Style." The main object was to be understood. Thus it was said that Mather "was very careful to be *understood,* and *concealed* every other *Art,* that he might Pursue and Practise that one *Art* of *Being Intelligible.*" He said of his own work that his *"Simple Discourses,* which they that account themselves the Wits of the World, look upon as *Babling,* will either be blessed by Christ for the Conversion and Edification of Souls, or turn for a Testimony to the Speaker."[36]

36. *Miller,* New England, p. 358.

Where Increase Mather kept to the plainness of style, Cotton Mather "bent toward rhetorical ornament and plentiful citation."[37] It is the number of "Authorities" which are quoted that is first noted in both tracts. While this procedure was common with the style of the day, one wonders if all the books were accessible to the Mathers at that time, or did they copy many of their quotations from other writers, as they give few citations for their references. Increase Mather could have easily copied most of his quotation from William Prynn's chapter against dancing in the *Histrio-Mastix.*[38] Prynn's chapter abounds in quotations, and he has footnotes for each.

37. *Ibid. p.* 353.

38. *William Prynne,* Histrio-Mastix *(London,* 1633), *Pt. I, p.* 220.

39. *Julius H. Tuttle, "The Libraries of the Mathers,"* Proceedings American Antiquarian Society, N.S. XX (1910), p. 287.

In checking into the library of the Mathers, a great number of the books quoted are listed as being there,[39] and many others were to be found in the community and at Harvard College.

It is interesting to note that throughout anti-dance literature, both before and after Mather's *Arrow*, most of the same citations are used. In later years, some were dropped as new writers wrote against dance. For example, Cotton Mather in *Clouds of Witnesses* uses almost all the same "authorities" as in the *Arrow*, yet he does not mention the *Arrow* or his father once.

The date of publication of Increase Mather's *Arrow*, as well as the number of editions printed, seems to have caused something of a puzzle.[40] Evens lists two editions: No. 370, with the imprint "Boston, Printed by Samuel Green and are to be sold by Joseph Brunning, 1684;" the other, No. 414, reading: "Boston, Printed by Richard Pierce, 1686." Despite this fact there was only one edition printed, and that was the one of 1685, misprinted 1684.

40. *For a greater discussion of the bibliographical data of Mathers'* Arrow; *see* Holmes, Increase Mather, *I, pp.* 20-26. *I have used Holmes as my source.*

As to the exact date, Sewall notes in his diary for Tuesday, February 16, 1685-6 (i.e. according to the old calendar 1685): "The Arrow against Dancing comes out." It was stated earlier the *Arrow* was written after the Stepney incident which was brought to court on November 12th, 1685, and therefore could not have been written at an earlier date. While the date 1684 is printed on the cover, it can be explained only as a misprint.

According to Holmes in *Increase Mather: A Bibliography,* he states that: "No copy of a second edition has ever come to light; no one has ever reported having seen a copy," and that the second edition seems to be a legend that has been perpetrated by bibliographers who did not check closely enough.

Nowhere in the *Arrow* or on the cover does it say that Increase Mather is the author. However, K.B. Murdock in his biography of Increase Mather quotes the following entry from Mather's diary: "This caused me to write that little discourse about profane and promiscuous dancing then printed." Cotton Mather in listing his father's works, lists the *Arrow* as being by his father and written in the year 1685.

Cotton Mather's *Cloud of Witnesses* was published anonymously and without imprint or date.[41] However, according to Holmes in *Cotton Mather: A Bibliography of His Works,* he states that ". . .the style reveals him [the author] to be Cotton Mather." The imprint that is given was assigned by Evens (921).

The work is very scarce. Holmes found

41. *I have used Holmes, Cotton Mather, A Bibliography of His Works (Cambridge, Mass., 1940), I, p. 157.*

only one copy, and that is the Yale University copy which I have used.

Increase Mather's *Arrow* and Cotton Mather's *Cloud of Witnesses* were only the beginning of a long list of tracts and sermons written against mixed dancing in the United States. The list grows, even today! Today, many not only agree with Mr. Moody that: " 'Twas not time for N.E. to dance" but that it is not time for the United States to dance!

PUBLISHER'S NOTE

The spelling, italization, punctuation
and capitalization for the *Arrow* and
Cloud of Witnesses follow those of
the original editions.

*An Arrow Against Profane and
Promiscuous Dancing Drawn out of the
Quiver of the Scriptures*

Title page of Increase Mather's *An Arrow*
Against Profane and Promiscuous Dancing
Courtesy The New York Public Library

An Arrow

AGAINST

Profane and Promiscuous

DANCING

Drawn out of the Quiver of the

SCRIPTURES.

By the Ministers of Christ at Boston
in New-England.

Judg. 6. 31. *Will you plead for Baal? Let
him plead for himself.*

*Chorea est Circulus cujus Centrum est
Diabolus.* Gulielm: Parisiensis.

Boston, *Printed by* Samuel Green, and
are to be Sold by *Joseph Brunning.*
1684

Increase Mather
Courtesy American Antiquarian Society

꾞 꾞 꾞 꾞 꾞 꾞 꾞 꾞 꾞 꾞 꾞 꾞 꾞 꾞 꾞 꾞 꾞 꾞

An Arrow against Mixt
D A N C I N G.

CONCERNING the Controversy about *Dancing*, the Question is not, whether all *Dancing* be in itself sinful. It is granted, that *Pyrrhical* or *Polemical Saltation:* i.e. where men vault in their Armour, to shew their strength and activity, may be of use. Nor is the question, whether a sober and grave *Dancing* of Men with Men, or of Women with Women, be not allowable; we make no doubt of that, where it may be done without offence, in due season, and with moderation. The Prince of Philosophers has observed truly, that *Dancing* or *Leaping,* is a natural expression of joy: So that there is no more Sin in it, than in laughter, or any outward expression of inward Rejoycing.

But our question is concerning *Gynecandrical Dancing,* or that which is commonly called *Mixt* or *Promiscuous Dancing, viz.* of Men and Women (be they elder or younger persons) together: Now this we affirm to be utterly unlawful, and that it cannot be tollerated in such a place as *New-England,* without great Sin. And that it may appear, that we are not transported by *Affection* without Judgment, let the following Arguments be weighed in the Ballance of the Sanctuary.

Arg. 1. *That which the Scripture condemns is sinful.* None but Atheists will deny this *Proposition:* But the Scripture condemns *Promiscuous Dancing.* This *Assumption* is proved, 1. *From the Seventh Commandment.*[1] It is an Eternal Truth to be observed in expounding the Commandment, that whenever any Sin is forbidden, not only the highest acts of that sin, but all degrees thereof, and all occasions leading thereto are prohibited. Now we cannot find one Orthodox and Judicious Divine, that writeth on the Commandments, but mentions *Promiscuous Dancing,* as a breach of the seventh Commandment, as being an occasion and an incentive to that which is evil in the sight of God. Yea, this is so manifest as that the *Assembly* in the *larger Catechism,* do expresly take notice of *Dancing,* as a violation of the Commandments. It is sad, that when in times of Reformations, Children have been taught in their Catechism, that such *Dancing* is against the Commandment of God, that now in *New-England* they should practically be learned the contrary. The unchast Touches and Gesticulations used by

1. *The Seventh Commandment states: "Thou shalt not commit adultery." Ex.* 20:14.

Dancers, have a palpable tendency to that which is evil. Whereas some object, that they are not sensible of any ill motions occasioned in them, by being Spectators or Actors in such *Saltations;* we are not bound to believe all which some pretend concerning their own Mortification. But suppose it were so, if there be other persons, who are by *Mixt Dancing* drawn into sin; that's enough against it. And that many are so, *Juvenal's*[2] Verses are a sufficient proof

Forsitan expectes ut [Gaditana] canoro Incipiat prurire choro, plausuq; probatae.[3]

And that of *Horace,*[4] *Motus doceri gaudet Jonicos Matura Virgo, & Fingitur Actibus, jam nunc & incestos amores, &c.*[5]

2. Besides the seventh Commandment, *There are other Scriptures, which seem expresly and particularly to condemn the Dancing we plead against.* It is spoken of as the great sin of the Daughters of *Sion,* that they did walk with stretched-out necks, and with wanton eyes, *walking and mincing as they go, and making a tinkling with their feet,* Isa. 3.16.[6] Those great Interpreters *Junius,*[7] and *Rivet,*[8] and *Ravanellus,*[9] conceive, that Scripture hath a special respect to those artificial and

2. *Juvenal (Decimus Junius Jubenalis) c. A.D. 60-140, a Roman satirical poet.*

3. *"You may look perhaps for a troop of Spanish maidens to win applause by immodest dance and song." Juvenal, Satire XI, line 162-3.*

4. *Horace (Quintus Horatius Flaccus); 65-8 B.C., Latin lyric poet.*

5. *"The maiden early takes delight in learning Grecian dances, and trains herself in coquetry e'en now, and plans unholy amours with passion unrestrained." Horace, Odes, Bk. III, lines 21-24.*

6. *Isa. 3:16. "The Lord also saith, Because ye daughters of Zion are haughty, and walk with stretched out necks, and with wandering eyes, walking and mincing as they go, and making a tinkling with their feet."*

7. *Junius, Francis (1545-1602) professor of divinity at Leyden.*

8. *Rivit (Andreas Rivetus, 1572-1651). A Huguenot, his important work being: Isagoge ad scripturam Sacrum Vetris et Novi Testamenti. Dort, 1616.*

9. *Ravanellus, Petrus (d.c. 1680) published: Bibliothica Sacra, seu Thesaurus Scripturae. Geneva, 1654.*

10. Rom. 13:13. "So that we walk honestly, as in the day: not in rioting and drunkenness, not in chambering and wantonness, not in strife and envying:"

11. I. Pet. 4:3. "For the time past of our life may suffice us to have wrought the will of the Gentiles, when we walk in lasciviousness, lust, excess of wine, revellings, banquetings, and abominable idolatries:"

12. Aretius, Benedictus, (1505-1574) a scientist and theologian, his chief work being: Theologioe Problemata (1573).

13. Voetius, Gisbert, (Gysbert Voet, 1589-1679), a Dutch Reformed theologian.

14. Hesychius, (6th, or 4th ? cent.), A Greek grammarian of Alexandria. He compiled a Greek lexicon.

15. Pindar, (522-c. 443 B.C.), generally regarded as the greatest Greek lyric poet.

proud carriages which are learned in the *Dancing School.* And the holy Apostle *Paul* condemns *Rioting* as a vice, *Rom.* 13.13.[10] The original word Critical and Accurate Expositors Interpret as reflecting on *Putulant Dancings.* And another Apostle speaks not only of *Excess in Wine,* but of *Revelling,* as a Sin which the Gentiles before their Conversion to Christ, were generally guilty of, I *Pet.* 4.3.[11] The word translated *Revelling,* may be read *Dancing.* It is the same with that in the *Romans,* which our translation calls *Rioting.* The learned *Aretius*[12] comments thus upon it; By κωμος, *he intends wanton Dancing, and so it is fitly mentioned after that of* Excess in Wine, *because it was customary with the Gentiles, after they had been drinking to Excess, to fall to dancing and singing; and commonly their Songs were profane and obscene.* Thus he, And indeed, as *Ravanellus* and *Voetius*[13] have well observed: the Greek work κωμος (which our Translators call *Rioting,* and in *Peter, Revelling)* is by the most learned in the Greek Tongue, judged to intend *Dancing.* Thus *Hesychius*[14] saith, that it is ειδος 'ορχησεως And it is evident, that *Pindar,*[15] the Greek Poet, doth so use the word. He saith, κωμαζε σὺν 'ὑμνω i.e. *Salta cum*

Hymno.[16] Vid. *Zuinger.*[17] *Theatr. Vol.* 2. lib.5. p. 389.

16. *dance with song.*

17. *Zuinger, Theodore,* (1534-1588), *a physician of Basil whose chief work is:* Theatrum Vitae Humanae. *Basil,* 1571.

The summe is, that according to the judgment of most profound and accurate Interpreters; the Scripture does expresly, and by name condemn *Dancing* as a vicious practice. The arguments stands thus, κωμοι are expresly condemned in the Scripture? But mixt *Dancings* are κωμοι, Therefore they are expresly condemned in the Scripture. Also under that of *Chambring, Wantonness, lascivousness* Dancings are implied.

3. *There are many other Scriptures which do implicitly condemn them as sinful.* How often does the Scripture commend unto Christians, *Gravity* and *Sobriety,* in their behaviour at all times; and condemn all *Levity* in Carriage. When as *Dancing* is (as some have expressed it) a *Regular Madness.* That wise Prince *Alphonsus,*[18] after he had seen such things, the question being asked, What is the difference between a *Dancer* and a *Mad-man?* Replied; *There was no other difference, but only this; that the person who is really* Phrentick, *is mad all the day long; when as the Dancer is only mad an hour in a day perhaps. Lud. Vives*[19] tells a pleasant story of certain men, who coming out of *Asia* into *Spain,* when they saw the *Spaniards* dance, they were so affrighted, as to run

18. *Prince Alphonsus,* (1396-1456), *a Spanish prelate and historian who succeeded his father as bishop of Burgos. His principal work is a history of Spain from the earlist times down to* 1496.

19. *Lud. Vives (Juan Ludovico Vives,* 1492-1540), *a learned and liberal-minded humanist of the* 16 *th century; a friend of Erasmus.*

away, supposing them to be possessed with some Spirit, or mad at least. And truly such affected Levity, and Antick Behaviour, when persons skip and fling about like *Bedlams,* as they say, *Dancers* are wont to do; is no way becoming the Gravity of a Christian. Moreover, the Scripture saith, *Whatsoever things are of good report,* think of these, *Phil.* 4.8.[20] which implieth, that Christians ought to avoid things of evil report. But *Promiscuous Dancings* are so; & that not only amongst serious Christians, but even amongst the Gentiles. Their grave and wise men have branded that custom as vile, infamous, and abominable; whose words we shall hear anon. But therefore that Rule which saith, meddle not with things of bad report, forbids Christians to have any concernment with *Promiscuous Dancings.* Yet again the Scripture saith, *Give no offence, neither to the Jew, nor to the Gentile, nor to the Church of God,* I Cor. 10.32.[21] In indifferent things this precept takes place; but the impleaded *Dancing* is very offensive upon more accounts than one, as will afterwards appear.

Arg. 2. *If we consider, by whom this practice of Promiscuous Dancing was first invented by whom patronized, and by whom witnessed against, we may well conclude, that the admitting of it, in such a place as*

20. Phil. 4:8. "Finally, brethren, whatsoever things are true, whatsoever things are honest, whatsoever things are just, whatsoever things are pure, whatsoever things are lovely, whatsoever things are of good report, if there be any virtue, if there be any praise, think on these things."

21. I Cor. 10:32. "Give none offence, neither to the Jew, nor to the Gentiles, nor to the church of God:"

New-England, *will be a thing pleasing to the Devil, but highly provoking to the Holy God.*

We design to write as comprehensively as we can; and have therefore in this Argument put several things together, the particulars wherof we shall endeavour to clear.

I. *Who were the Inventors of Petulant Dancings?* They had not their original amongst the People of God, but amongst the Heathen. Learned men have well observed, that the Devil was the first inventor of the impleaded *Dances,* and the Gentiles, who worshiped him, the first Practitioners in this Art. They did honour the Devils, whom they served in this way; their Festivals being for the most part spent in Play and Dances. And from them did the Apostatizing Idolatrous *Israelites* learn to behave themselves, as they did, when they worshipped the Golden Calf. *They sat down, to eat and drink, and rose up to play,* or to dance. I *Cor.* 7.10.[22] Hence amongst the Greeks, *Bacchus* was stiled Θεος χορειος; the God that loved Dancing. Their manner was, that a Company of Young Men and Women, with Musical Instruments, would Dance and Sing together, in honour of *Bacchus;* whom also they called by the name of Κωμος which (as before was shewed) does from thence signifie *Dancing.* vid. *Alting*[23] *Theol. Problem.*

22. I *Cor.* 7:10. *The printer or Mather has made an error, it should read I Cor.* 10:7. *"Neither be ye idolaters, as were some of them; as it is written, The people sat down to eat and drink, and rose up to play."*

23. *Alting, Johann Heinrich, (1583-1644), was a German Protestant theologion, professor of dogma at Heidelberg and later of theology at Groningen.*

24. *Strabo, (63 B.C.-24 A.D.) was a celebrated Greek geographer. I cannot find in Strabo lib. 13 or elsewhere in Strabo that apes were taught to dance.*

25. *Jer.* 10:2. *"Thus saith the Lord, Learn not the way of the heathen, and be not dismayed at the signs of heaven; for the heathen are dismayed at them."*

26. *Lev.* 20:23. *"And ye shall not walk in the manner of the nations which I cast out before you: for they committed all these things, and therefore I abhorred them."*

27. *I Pet.* 1:18. *"Forasmuch as ye know that ye were not redeemed with corruptible things, as silver and gold, from your vain conversation received by tradition from your fathers;"*

28. *Rom.* 12:2. *"And be not conformed to this world; but be ye transformed by the renewing of your mind, that ye may prove what is that good, and acceptable, and perfect will of God."*

29. *Caligula, (Caius Caesar, 12-41 A.D.) was the third emperor of Rome, 37-41 A.D. Noted for his infamous reign.*

30. *Nero, (Nero Claudius Caesar Drusus Germanieus, 37-68 A.D.), was emperor of Rome from 54-68 A.D. Noted for his infamous reign.*

31. *Epicures, (342-270 B.C.), taught that pleasure is the only possible end of rational action, and that the*

Loc. 10. p. 510. Nor is it to be wondred that those miserably deluded Souls, who thought and taught, that their Gods were Adulterers, did suppose that they would be delighted with such Dances; as had a tendency that way, yea, the Gentiles took such pleasure in Dancing, that they learned some irrational Creatures that foolish Art. In special (as *Strabo*[24] *in lib.* 13. relates) they taught *Apes* to Dance. When *Diana's* Festival was celebrated, *Dancing Apes* were brought fourth to honour it. This is enough to make Christians, not only deride, but detest such Vanities; especially considering that the Scripture saith, *Learn not the way of the Heathen.* Jer. 10.2.[25] And that the Lord's People may *not do after their manners,* nor imitate their Heathenish Customes, *Lev.* 20.23.[26] And that Christ came to redeem Believers from their *vain Conversation,* I Pet. 1.18.[27] And that they should not *be conformed to this world,* Rom. 12.2.[28]

A practice in use, only amongst the Heathen, but never known among the people of God, except in times of degeneracy, ought not to be taken up. But this is true of that practice, which we now testify against.

2. *By whom have Promiscuous Dances been patronized?* Truly, by the worst of the Heathen. *Caligula,*[29] *Nero,*[30] and such like Atheists and Epicures[31] were delighted in

them. *Lucius*[32] (that infamous Apostate) hath written an Oration, in defence of profane and Promiscuous Dancings. Amongst the Papists, some of their more grave Writers, decry such a practice as a great Immorality. *Alexander Fabritius,*[33] a Learned Man, though Popishly affected, was indeed clearly convinced of the great sin which is therein. His words are worthy our taking notice of them; he thus expresseth himself. *The entring into the Processions of Dances, hinders men from ingress into the heavenly Procession; and those who Dance, offend against the Sacraments of the Church. First, against Baptism; They break the Covenant which they made with God in Baptism; wherein they promised, to renounce the Devil and his Pomps; but when they enter into the Dance, they go in the Pompous Procession of the Devil.* Thus that Author: But generally, Popish Casuists justify it, as they do many other moral evils; so *Cajetan*[34] *Azorius,*[35] *Silvester,*[36] and other Papists: The corrupt Schoolmen[37] makes a light matter of it, calling it a *Venial Sin.* And therefore *Lavater*[38] does justly unbraid the Popish Religion, in that their Writers do generally maintain the lawfulness of *Promiscuous Dancings.* So that the Patrons of this Practice are men not *sound in the Faith.*

ultimate pleasure is freedom.

32. Lucius was probably Lucian of Samosata (b. c.120 A.D.) the famous satirist. His famous work on the dance is titled: Of Pantomime. William Smith and Henry Wace, A Dictionary of Christian Biography (London, 1882) state: "Some writers have represented him as an apostate from Christianity; this is, however, very improbable, and rests on no good authority."

33. Alexander Fabritius, (Andreas Fabricius, 1520-1581), was a Roman Catholic divine.

34. Cajitan, Thomas DeVio, (1469-1534), an Italian Cardinal and scholar who summoned Luther before his tribunal.

35. Azorius, (Juan Azor, 1535-1603), was a member of the Society of Jesus.

36. Silvester, (Sylvester II, d.1003), was Pope (999-1003), a Frenchman.

37. Schoolmen were teachers of philosophy and theology at the medieval universities, then usually called 'schools' of which Paris and Oxford were pre-eminent. From the 13th century, many of the greatest representatives belong to the Medicant Orders, among the most famous being the Dominicans St. Albert the Great, and St. Tomas Aquinas, and the Franciscans St. Bonaventure and Duns Scotus.

38. Lavater, Louis,

(1527-1586), was a Swiss Protestant theologian.

3. *Who are they that have faithfully testified against this practice?* Ignorant and Profane Men say, no body is against it, but a few silly Precisians, who are more precise than wise. But we certainly know, that the wisest, and the learnedest, and the holiest men in the world have disliked it. *The Ancient Doctors,* (Fathers as they are called) have thundred against this Sin. *Chrysostom*[39] in his Sermons on *Genesis*, treating on *Jacob's* Marriage; *Here* (saith he) *We read of a Wedding, but not a word of Dancing there.* Yea, he sticks not to call *Dancing* a *Diabolical Practice.* And in another of his Sermons; He saith, that *Wherever this is a Petulant Dance, the Devil is one of the Company. And Arnobius*[40] does vehemently reprehend the Gentiles, because of their lascivious Dances. *Austin*[41] doth severely tax this vice. *Ambrose*[42] doth advise all Godly Parents, that would not have the Souls of their Children corrupted and ruined, not to send them to the Dancing-School. And how often do the Fathers call the *Dance a Work of Satan, one of his Pomps and Vanities, which all baptized persons are bound to renounce?* And not only Fathers, but whole *Councils* have born witness against them. So did the *Oecumenical* Synod at *Constaninople.* Also the Synod which met at *Laodicea,* and several others,

39. Chrysostom, St. John, (347?-407), was a celebrated father of the Greek church. He was cannonized by both the Greek and Catholic church.

40. Arnobius (surnamed Afer, c.300 A.D.), was a rhetorician and Christian apologist. His chief work being: Against the Gentiles.

41. Austin — An older English form of Augstine or St. Augustine.

42. Ambrose, St., (340?-397), Bishop of Milan and one of the greatest Fathers of the Church.

absolutely prohibit all Promiscuous Dancings, not allowing them so much, as at Weddings. Thus it was with Christians, before the World did degenerate again into Paganish, Heathenish Customs. We have now heard the ordinance of Antiquity discharged against the impleaded Dancers. A Shower of Arrows are yet behind.

As for *the great Reformers of Religion, and Opposers of Antichristianism,* none have gone beyond them, in an Holy Zeal against Profane and Promiscuous Dancing. Let us in the first place, cite the *Waldenses:*[43] They are in the Scripture, honoured with the name of *Saints,* Rev. 13.7.[44] These *Saints of God,* and *Martyrs of Jesus,* were haters of Mixt Dances. Because their words are Pathetical; we shall here transcribe and insert them, as we find them mentioned by *Perrin,*[45] in his History of the Doctrine and Discipline of the *Waldenses,* p. 63. They thus testify: *A Dance is the Devils Procession. He that enters into a Dance, enters into his Possession. The Devil is the Guide, the middle and the end of the Dance. A man sinneth in Dancing divers wayes; as in his Pace, for all his steps are numbered; in his Touch, in his Ornaments, in his Hearing, sight, Speech, and other Vanities. We will prove first from Scripture, and then by other Reasons, how wicked a thing it is*

43. *According to Perrin (see below) the Waldenses were, "Luther's forerunners — who for divers hundred years before Luther successively opposed Popery, professed the truth of the Gospell and sealed it with their blood."*

44. *Rev. 13:7. "And it was given unto him to make war with the saints, and to overcome them: and power has given him over all kindreds, and tongues, and nations."*

45. *Perrin, Jean Paul, (16th cent.) was a French historian.*

{ 41 }

to Dance.—*He that Danceth maintaineth the Devil's Pomp, and singeth his Mass. Again, In a Dance, a man breaks the Ten Commandments of God. The very motion of the Body, which is used in Dancing, giveth Testimony enough of evil.* Austin *saith, The miserable Dancer knoweth not, that as many Paces as he makes in Dancing, so many steps he makes to Hell.* Thus (and much more to this purpose) do those faithful Witnesses of Christ, declare against this Profane Practice. Moreover, the Ministers of the *Reformed Churches in France*, did above an hundred years ago, (*viz.Anno* 1581) concur in writing, and publishing a Book, against the vice we are impleading. Also Venerable *Calvin;*[46] *Marlorat,*[47] *Lavater, Danaeus,*[48] *Tilenus,*[49] *Polanus,*[50] *Zepperus;*[51] all condemn it as utterly unlawful. *Peter Martyr*[52] and *Aretius* in their common places, do elaborately discourse about mixed Dancing, and prove it to be an unlawful Recreation. The Judicious *Rivet* saith, that such Dancings as teach wantonness in looks, or pride in behaviour, as he thinks almost all the *Saltations* do, which are now adayes Artificially learned in the *Dancing-Schools*, are breaches of the seventh Commandment, and ought not to be tolerated in any Christian Common-wealth. The great

46. *Calvin, John, (1509-1564), was a celebrated Protestant reformer and theologian, the founder of Calvinism which included election or predestination, limited atonment, total depravity, irresistibility of grace, and the perseverance of the saints. The sovereignty of God in the bestowal of grace was greatly emphasized.*

47. *Marlorat, Augustine, (1506-1563), was a French Protestant theologin.*

48. *Danaeus, (Daneau) Lambert, (1530-1595), was an eminent French Protestant theologian who wrote: Trait des Danse, Auquel est Amplement Resolue la Question, Assouoir s'il est Permis aux Chretiens de Danser. (Geneve, 1579).*

49. *Tilenus, Daniel, (1563-1633), was a learned French divine.*

50. *Polanus, Amandus, (1561-1610), was professor of divinity at Basil.*

51. *Zepperus, (Zepper, Wilhelm, 1550-1607), was a Dutch Protestant theologian.*

52. *Peter Martyr, (Pietro Martire d'Anghiera, 1457-1526), was an Italian courtier, geographer and historian.*

{ 42 }

Voetius hath lately, and (according to his wonted manner) with very much learning and strength of reason, proved that such Exercises are very sinful. The like has been done by the Excellent *Altingius.* Amongst our *English* Divines there is *a cloud of Witnesses.* There are three *Bishops* who have written against Promiscuous *Dancing* as unlawful; so Dr. *Downham,*[53] *Babington*[54] and *Andrews,*[55] and one *Arch-Bishop* (tho we confess a Puritanical one) *viz.* the incomparable *Usher,*[56] hath given his Testimony against Vanities of this kind. Besides these Dr. *Rainold,*[57] Dr. *Ames,*[58] Mr. *Perkins,*[59] Mr. *Dod,*[60] Mr. *Elton,*[61] Mr. *Bolton,*[62] Mr. *Brinsley,*[63] Mr. *Durham*[64] and others have abundantly proved it to be unlawful. Also Mr. *Prin*[65] has in his *Histrio Mastix,* a large discourse on this subject. Whoso shall please to read him, will find that good men have been very severe in their cencure on *Dancers.* He will there see it affirmed, that *mixed Dancing is a Recreation fitter for Pagans & whores & Drunkards than for Christians:* And that the Gate of Heaven is too strait for a *Chore* of impure Dancers to enter in thereat: & that such *Capring Goats* will not be found amongst Sheep at the last Day, with many the like severe expressions. So odious was this practice in former times,

53. Downham (Downame), John, (1571?-1643), was an English Bishop and author of popular expositions of Puritan doctrine.

54. Babington, Gervase, (1550-1610), was Bishop of Worcester.

55. Andrews, Lancelot, (1555-1626), was an English prelate and author, dean of Westminster, Bishop of Chichester, Ely, Winchester and one of the translators of the King James version of the Bible.

56. Usher, James, (1581-1656), was a British prelate, theologian, and scholar. He was Arch-bishop of Armagh and primate of Ireland in 1624 or 1625.

57. Rainhold (Reynolds), John, (1549-1607), was president of Corpus College, Oxford and Dean of Lincoln. He was appointed by King James to be one of the translators of the Bible, but died before its completion.

58. Ames, William, (1576-1633). was an English Puritan theologian and casuist residing in the Netherlands.

59. Perkins, William, (1558-1602), Puritan nonconformist and theological writer and preacher, he taught at Cambridge.

60. Dod, John, (1550-1646), was a Puritan divine.

61. Elton, Edward, (d. 1624), was an English theologian.

62. Bolton, Robert, (1572-1631), was a Puritan divine.

63. Brinsley, John, the elder, (fl. 1633), also John the younger. Both were Puritan divines, the elder being an educational writer.

64. Durham, James, (1622-1658), was an English Covenanting divine.

65. Prin (Prynne), William, (1600-1669), a Puritan pamphleteer.

66. Rom. 2:14,15. "For when the Gentiles, which have not the law, do by nature things contained in the law, these, having not the law, are a law unto themselves: Which show the work of the law written in their hearts, their conscience also bearing witness, and their thoughts the mean while accusing or else excusing one another."

67. Macrobius, (fl. c. 400) was a Latin writer and philospher; noted for his book Saturnalia, which is a source of quotations from early writers.

68. Scipio Africanus, Minor, (c.185-129 B.C.) is celebrated in Cicero's De Amicitia. He is quoted here from Macrobius's Saturnalia lib.2, chap.XI.

69. Salust (Sallust), (86-34 B.C.), was a Roman historian.

70. Salust writes about Sempronia in The Conspiracy of Catiline Chap. XXV. "Among

when Debauchery and Atheism had not obtained that Credit which this Adulterous Generation has put upon it.

Arg. 3. *That Practice which the Graver sort of Heathen have condemned as unlawful, Christians may well look upon as Sinful,* Rom. 2.14,15.[66] *But this is true concerning mixed Dancing;* as shall by Testimony be made to appear.

Macrobius[67] informs us, that amongst the Ancient *Romans* skil in Dancing was reputed an infamous thing. *Scipio Africanus*[68] complains that some in his time would go with *impudent Dancers* (as he calls them) and learn to sing with them, Which practice their Ancestors looked upon as a disgrace to Gentlemen. He therefore speaks of it as a great degeneracy of that Age, that some being Persons of Quality, sent their Children to a Dancing-school, and that he had himself seen at one of their Schools, a Boy of twelve years old Dancing, which he thought was a fitter employment for a lewd and foolish serving-boy, than for the Son of a Gentleman. And *Salust*[69] (that brave *Roman* Historian) layeth it as a Brand of Infamy upon *Sempronia,*[70] that she had been taught to *Dance,* which he says was a sign of dishonesty; such a practice being *the instrument of Luxury.* And *Cicero*[71] in his Oration *Pro Muræna*[72] saith, that if a Man be a

{ 44 }

Dancer, he is doubtless either a Drunkard or a mad man. *Nemo saltat sobrius nisi forte insaniat.* He blames *Cato* for having such hard thoughts of *Muræna,* as to suppose him guilty of *Dancing.* For (saith he) if he be a *Dancer,* without doubt he is a bad man indeed, since that Vice never goeth alone. He saith of *Gabinius* and *Antonius* that they must needs be vicious persons, because they were *Dancers. Seneca*[73] bewails it, that in his time young Ones were corrupted with *Obscene Dances;* and that *Dancing-schools* were tolerated in the City, and that some when they were inflamed at the *Dance,* went from the *Dancing-school* to the *Brothel house. Priamus*[74] severly reproved his sons because he understood they were 'ορχησται i.e. *Dancers, Plutarch*[75] in his Description of a Vertuous Woman, mentions this as a Negative qualification, that she must not be a Dancer. Understand him and the other Authors cited, as speaking of Promiscuous *Dances.* The Emperor *Tiberius*[76] banished *Dancers,* not only from his Court, but out of the City of *Rome.*

Now then, shall the *Gentiles,* who had only the dark Light of Nature to shew them what things were good & what evil; condemn *Petulant dancings?* And shall Christians who have the Scriptures and the Glorious Light of the Gospel to il-

these women was a Sempronia who had perpetrated many crimes, often worthy of a man's daring. She was well endowed with birth and beauty, and fortunate in her husband and children; was well read in Greek and Latin literature, could sing play, and dance more gracefully than an honest woman need, and had many other accomplishments of a riotous life."

71. Cicero, Marcus Tullius, (106-43 B.C.), was celebrated as a Roman orator, philosopher, and statesman.

72. "For almost no one dances when he is sober—except perhaps a lunatic—nor when he is alone nor at a staid and respectable feast." Pro Muræna VI. p. 13.

73. Seneca, Lucius Annaeus, (c.3B.C.-A.D. 65), was a Roman philosopher, dramatist, and statesman.

74. Priam in Greek legend, Trojan king; husband of Hecuba and father of Hector, Paris, Troilus, Cassandra and others. Homer in the Iliads (bk.24 1.256-259) has Priam say:". . . .These are gone, you that survive are base, Liers and common free-booters, all faultie, not at grace but in your heels in all your parts; dancing companions, yet all are excellent."

75. Plutarch, (A.D. 46?-c. 120) Greek biographer and essayist.

76. Tiberius (42

B.C.-A.D.37), Roman emperor A.D. 14-37. Suetonius in his life of Tiberius says (par.36) "The theatre audience had formed factions in support of rival actors, [dancers] and once when their quarrels ended in bloodshed, Tiberius exiled not only the factions leaders but the actors who had been the occasion of the riot; nor would he ever give way to popular entreaties by recalling them." Graves trans.

luminate them, practise or plead for such works of Darkness? And shall that *Abomination* be set up in *New-England* (the place where the Light of the Gospel has shined so Gloriously) which *Moral Heathen* have detested? The Lord lay not this great sin to the charge of any, who have at all been guilty of it.

Arg. 4. *The practice which is not sanctified by Prayer, but is an Enemy to Religious Exercises, is surely an evil Practice. But this is true concerning mixt dancing.* It is a good Rule which *Practical and Casuistical* Divines are wont to give, *That work which a Man cannot pray over, let him not meddle with.* A Christian should do nothing wherein he cannot exercise Grace, or put a respect of Obedience to God on what he does. This in lawful Recreations may be done. 1 *Cor.*

77. 1 Cor. 10:31. "Whether therefore ye eat, or drink, or whatsoever ye do, do all to the glory of God."

10.31.[77] But who can seriously pray to the Holy God to be with him when he is going to a Promiscuous *dance?* It is that which hinders Religious Exercises, especially for persons to go immediately from hearing a Sermon to a *Gunecandrical Dance.* It is a high degree of profaneness, and impudent contempt put upon the Gospel. The Devil thereby catcheth away the good seed of the Word, and the former Religious Exercise is rendered ineffectual. Some that write against *dances,* observe, that many young persons who seemed to be hopeful, and to have some good beginnings of Piety in them, by falling into acquaintance with that unlawful Recreation, have in a little time utterly left all favour of good; it being just with God, when they have forsaken him to follow the Devils Pomps and Vanities, to withdraw his Holy Spirit from them, and judicially give them up to mind nothing else but Folly. The Lord grant that none amongst our selves may find the observation true.

Arg. 5. For Persons to Dance at a Time when God calls them to mourn, is certainly unlawful. But such is the case at this Day. If the thing were in it self lawful (which the Arguments insisted on prove that it is not) yet to set upon such a practice at such a time, must needs be a great provocation to the sight of God. *Dancers* are wont to alledge that Scripture, *Eccl.* 3.4.[78] *There is a Time to Dance,* (though that does not speak a syllable for the Justification of such *Dancing* as we are writing against, nor indeed for any other *Dancing,* since the meaning of the place is not that there is a *lawful time,* but only a *limited time* to Dance.) But they should consider that *There is a Time*

78. *Eccl.* 3:4 "A time to weep, and a time to laugh; a time to mourn, and a time to dance;"

{ 47 }

79. Jer. 9:20. "Yet hear the word of the Lord, O ye women, and let your ears receive the word of his mouth, and teach your daughters wailing, and every one her neighbour lamentation."

80. Amos 6:5. "That chant to the sound of the viol, and invent to themselves instruments of music, like David.

81. Ezek. 21:10. "It is sharpened to make a sore slaughter; it is furbished that it may glitter: should we then make mirth? it contemneth the rod of my son, as every tree."

to mourn. Now to set up *Dances* at a Time when God calls to mourn, is most certainly a provocation. There was a Time when God by his Prophet said, *Hear the Word of the Lord, O ye Women, and teach your daughters wailing,* Jer. 9.20.[79] And so does he speak by his providence at this day: But at a Time when God saith, *Teach your Daughters wailing,* shall we say *no, We will teach them Dancing?* There is a word pronounced upon them that are at ease in Sion, and who at a season when they should be grieved for the Affliction of *Joseph,* are *Chanting to the sound of the Viol,* Amos 6.5.[80] Every body knows that it is a time of much Affliction with the Church of God in the World. They that begin a *Dance* now, give but a poor evidence of their belonging to the Mystical Body of Christ, when they do no more sympathize with its sorrow. Is this a Time for *Jigs* and *Galiards!* Let us recommend to such persons the serious Consideration of that Scripture, *Isa.* 22. 12,13,14. *In that Day did the Lord God of Hosts call to weeping and to mourning. And behold Joy and Gladness, Let us Eat and Drink, for to morrow we shall Die. It was revealed in mine Ears by the Lord of Hosts, surely this Iniquity shall not be purged from you till you Die, saith the Lord of Hosts.* The Judgments of God are abroad in the World, and hanging over our own heads too. *Should we then make Mirth? Ezek.* 21.10.[81] Blessed Mr. *Cotton,*[82] tho he be dead (and hath been for 33 years) yet speaketh. He hath left behind him this Testimony (in his Book on *Eccl.* 3.4.) *To Dance though at Marriages is unmeet, especially in* N.E. *And at such a Time as this, when the Churches are in Distress.*[83] Should he rise out of his Tomb (which is here amongst us) how would his Holy Soul be grieved to behold such Degeneracy in this *Boston.*

Arg. 6. *That Practice against which the wrath of God hath been revealed from Heaven, may well be dreaded as unrighteous.* Rom. 1.18.[84] *But this is sadly true concerning mixt Dancings.* The Fruits and Effects thereof have been Tragical & Dismal. No doubt but that the *Promiscuous Dances* (for at their Sacrifices the Heathen used to do so) between the *Moabites* and the *Midianitish* Woman, proved a snare to the Children of *Israel.* But how terrible a Plague followed? *Rivet, Ravanellus* and others conclude that *Dinah*[85] went to see a *Dance* among the *Shechemites;* if her good Father had not indulged her that liberty, he had saved her from Ruine, and himself and

82. *Cotton, John,* (1585-1652), *was a Puritan clergyman who emigrated from England and settled in Boston, Massachusetts. He was called "the Patriarch of New England."*

83. *John Cotton writing on Eccl.* 3:4 *says: "To take off the plea for dancing hence. For it is not said there is a lawful time to dance, but a limited time. Herodias' daughter (Salome) had a time to dance, as to earn halfe a Kingdome for a dance, and to get John Baptist's head; So another time of a contrary dance, when falling through the Ice (if we may believe Nicephorus, lib. I. cap.*20) *her feet capered under water, and her head being cut off by the Ice, it danced above the Ice. We read First, of a Religious dance, Exod.* 15.20, *Secondly, of a civil dance to entertaine Conquerours,* Judg. 11.44, I Sam. 18.6, Luke 15.25, *when the eyes are set upon joy. But, not in marriages, where is more temtation to lust. Tully pro Murana! Nemo saltat sobrius nisi forte insaniat, neque solitudine neque in convivio honesto & moderato especially it unmeet in N.E. and now when the Church of England are in such distress, Ezek.* 21.10." (p.58)

84. Rom. 1:18. *"For the wrath of God is revealed from heaven against all ungodliness and unrighteousness of men, who hold the truth in unrighteousness."*

85. *While Rivet, Ravanellus and others may conclude that Dinah*

went to see a dance I can find nothing in the Bible that states such. Gen. 34:1,2. "And Dinah the daughter of Leah, which she bare unto Jacob, went out to see the daughters of the land.
"And when Shechem the son of Hamor the Hivite, prince of the country, saw her, he took her, and lay with her, and defiled her." The rest of the story is told in verses 3-31, but not a word is mentioned about dance.

86. Mat. 14:6,7,8. "But when Herod's birthday was kept, the daughter of Herodias danced before them, and pleased Herod. Whereupon he promised with an oath to give her whatever she would ask. And she, being before instructed of her mother, said Give me here John Baptist's head in a charger."

87. Nicephorus, (c. 758-829), celebrated Byzantine historian and patriarch of Constantinople.

88. Beard, Thomas, (d. 1632), was a Doctor of Divinity, Puritan divine and school master of Oliver Cromwell.

89. Numb. 16:30. "but if the Lord make a new thing, and the earth open her mouth, and swallow them up, with all that appertain unto them, and they go down quick into the pit; then ye shall understand that these men have provoked the Lord."

Family from great Reproach. *Salome*,[86] the Daughter of *Herodias* was notable at *Dancing!* But what end did she come to? *Nicephorus*[87] relates that falling under the Ice, her feet *Capered* under the water; and her Head being cut off by the Ice, it danced above water. The Story of that Bishop is famous, who having a Mixed Dance in his House, he and the female in his hand hapned to be crush'd to Death. Also in the City of *Magdeburg*, 24 Persons (Men and Women) were struck dead with the Lightnings as they were *Promiscuously Dancing*. See Dr. *Beard's*[88] *Theater of Judgments*, Chap. 36. Hereby may we understand that such Men have provoked the Lord, *Numb.* 16.30.[89] Histories have many other tragical stories confirming this Argument, which we forbear to mention. It is known from their own Confessions that amongst the *Indians* in this *America*, oftentimes at their *Dances* the Devil appears in bodily shape, and takes away one of them alive. In some places of this Wilderness there are great heaps of Stones, which the *Indians* have laid together, as an horrid Remembrance of so hideous a fruit of their *Satanical Dances*. The Writer of *Magica de Spectris*, observes, That there was hardly any meeting betwixt the Devil and Witches wherein there was no *Dancing.*

But let us hear what the Patrons of Dances have to plead. *Produce your Cause, and bring forth your strong Reasons, saith the Lord.* Say all that you have to say.

Plea. 1. *We Read in the Scripture of* Dances. *Miriam Danced,*[90] and *David Danced.*[91]

Answ. 1. Those Instances are not at all to the purpose; for they were Religious *Dances,* accommodated to the State of the Old Testament-Church. They had also Music in their worship, but such as have so in these dayes *Judaize* more than *Christians* ought to do, we should divert into another *Question,* should we speak to that.

2. Neither were those mentioned, *Mixed dancings:* It is said of *Miriam, The Woman went out after her with Dances, Exod.* 15.20. But not that Men went out with them: Nor did *David* take a Woman by the hand to *Dance* with him before the Ark. In one Word, there is not so much as one Example in the whole Book of God concerning *mixt dancing,* except it be the Instance of that accursed and damned Harlot the Daughter of *Herodias.*

90. *Ex.* 15:20. "And Miriam the prophetess, the sister of Aaron, took a timbrel in her hand; and all the women went out after her with timberls and with dances."

91. 2 *Sam.* 6:16. "And as the ark of the LORD came into the city of David, Michal, Saul's daughter, looked through a window, and saw king David leaping and dancing before the LORD; and she despised him in her heart."

Plea. 2. *The Design of Dancing is only to teach Children good Behaviour and decent Carriage.*

Ans. Religion is no Enemy to good Manners, to learn a due Poyse and Composure of Body is not unlawful, provided it be done without a provocation to Uncleanness, and be not a Nurse of Pride and Vanity. If therefore any be disposed to have their Children instructed in that which may be truly Ornamental, or a desirable Accomplishment in these respects, they may send them not to a Blasphemer, but to some Grave Person that will teach them Decency of Behaviour, not *Promiscuously,* but each Sex by themselves; so neither God nor Man will be offended.

This notwithstanding, Every thing is not *Good Carriage;* which Light and Vain Persons shall call so. Why should *Pantomimical Gestures* be named good Carriage. There is a behaviour which Light Persons look upon as an accomplishment; but such as are grave and solid, and wise (whose esteem is most to be valued) have other thoughts of it. If the Holy Prophet *Isaiah* were alive in these dayes, he would not call a *stretched forth neck, and wanton eye, a Mincing as they go,* by the name of good carriage. It is one of the Devil's Wiles to Guild over corrupt Practices with Golden Names, that men may the more easily swallow them. In this debauched Age; frequent *Osculations* amongst those that are not in any Conjugal Relation, is called good Breeding, Gentile behaviour, and the like. But Christians ought to hate such tendencies to *Nicolaitism*,[92] for Christ hates them, *Rev.* 2.6.[93]

Plea. 3. *Children are much pleased with this Exercise.* Ans. That we believe: But if it suit with their corrupt natures, that's a sign it is evil. No doubt but if a Stage play were set up, many Children would be as much pleased with it, as now they are with the Dance. If a Blasphemer shall tell them, There's as good Divinity to be learned by a Play as by the Scripture it self, perhaps they may be debauched into the belief of it, if ever they should see Scripture-stories acted in a Play, which indeed is a profane Practice common amongst the Papists, but prohibited in Reformed Churches under pain of the highest censure. The Lord saith, *Seek not after your own heart and your own wayes,* after which you use to go an whoring, *Numb.* 15.35.[94]

Plea. 4. *Such dancing is now become customary amongst Christians. Ans.* Which cannot be thought on without hor-

92. *Nicolaitism is a sect mentioned in the Apocalypse or Revelations. It was said they led lives of unrestrained indulgence.*

93. *Rev.* 2:6. *"But this thou hast, that thou hatest the deeds of the Nicolaitanes, which I also hate." also Rev.* 2:15. *"So hast thou also them that hold the doctrine of the Nicolaitanes, which thing I hate."*

94. *Numb.* 15:35. *"And the Lord said to Moses, The man shall surely be put to death; all the congregation shall stone him with stones without the camp."*

{ 53 }

ror. A great and Learned Divine takes notice of it as a very sad thing, that all the profane Dances in use amongst the Lascivious Greeks of Old, have of late years been revived in the Christian World; yea, and in Places where the Reformed Religion has taught men better. But shall Christian follow the course of the World? They ought to swim against the stream, and to keep themselves pure from the sins of the Times of which this of *mixed dancing* is none of the least.

Plea. 5. *Some good men think it is lawful! Ans.* We are not to walk by the Opinion of this or that good Man, but by the Scriptures. *To the Law and to the Testimony, if they speak not according to that there is no light in them.* Fearful Judgments have befallen a Professing People for doing such things as some good Men through error of Judgment have approved of. We dare not deny, that there have been some good Men in the world, who have been so far misled as to justify Profanations of the Lords Day. And *Lutherans* have pleaded for Graven Images, contrary to the second Commandment. But should such things be tolerated in *N.E.* we have reason to believe that the hot displeasure of God would soon burn against us. Besides, it is more than we know, if one good man hath written in defence of mixt Dancings. One that hath written against Dancers, giveth his Book this Title, *The Church of ungodly Men and Women whose King is Lucifer.*[95] But we cannot call to mind one Protestant Author who has been real for the interest of Reformation, that has set his Pen on work to plead for a practice so vile and infamous. This Objection turns upon Dancers thus, That practice with Holy Men in all ages have abhorred may well be suspected to be an evil practice: But it was shewed that this is true of promiscuous Dancing. We shall then conclude this Discourse with a double *Corollary.*

Corol. I. *It is the Duty of Churches to exercise the Discipline of Christ towards such of their Members as shall offend in this matter.* The Rule is clear and written with the Beams of the Sun, 2 *Thes.* 3.6. *We command you, Brethren, in the Name of our Lord Jesus Christ, that you withdraw your selves from every Brother that walketh disorderly, and not after the Tradition which he received from us.* Now they that frequent Promiscuous Dancings, or that send their Children thereunto, walk disorderly, and contrary to the Apostles Doctrine. It has been proved that such a practice is a *Scandalous*

95. *The book is mentioned in William Prynn's* Histrio Mastix, *Part I, Actus 5, Scena 8. He lists it as being printed by Richard Pinson.*

{ 55 }

Immorality, and therefore to be removed out of Churches by Discipline, which is the Broom of Christ, whereby he keeps his Churches clean. *Zepperus* and others observe that it was by this means, that Churches in the Primitive times were preserved from this corruption. And thus it hath been in the Reformed Churches. The National Synod held at *Dort,* Anno 1578. thus express themselves, *Because Dances are for the most part attended with a Levity unbecoming Christians, and are an offence to the Godly, especially when practiced in a time of common Danger and Calamity, they that go to Dances, shall be reproved, and if after divers Admonitions they persist therein, they are to be excluded from Communion.* And several Provincial Assemblies in *Holland,* have declared that the sword of Discipline ought to be brandished again such Offenders, as *Voetius* testifieth *(In Disput, de exelsis mundi,* p. 346,347.) And the *Reforming Synods* in *Poland* above an hundred years ago, did absolutely prohibit these Dances, and prescribe the use of Discipline against that evil: Once more in the printed Discipline of the Reformed Churches in *France,* p.45. They have this Article, *Dancing is to be suppressed, and those that take the liberty or custom to Dance after they have been several times Admonished shall be Excommunicated, when they shew themselves obstinate in their Rebellion. And the Consistories are exhorted well to put this Article into Execution, and to read the same publickly in the Name of God, and in the Authority of the Synod, and the said Synod and Conferences are exhorted to take heed of and warn those Consistories that therein do not their Duties, to censure the Offenders for it.*

And shall Churches in *N.E.* who have had a Name to be stricter and purer than other Churches, suffer such a scandalous evil amongst them? if all that are under Discipline be made sensible of this matter, we shall not be much or long infested with a *Choreutical Dæmon.*

Corol. 2. *Such Church-Members in* N.E., *as have sent their Children to be Practitioners or Spectators of mixt Dancing between young Men and Maidens, have cause to be deeply humbled.* But stand still a while! what a word is here! *Church-Members and their Children in* N.E. *at mixt Dances! Be astonished O ye Heavens!* without doubt *Abraham is ignorant of us, and Israel knoweth us not.* If our Fathers should rise out of their Graves, they would not own such Children. It has been observed by several learned & holy Men that *Job* giveth it as the Description and Character of ungodly ones: *They send forth their little ones like a Flock, and their Children Dance, they take the Timbrel and Harp, and rejoyce at the sound of the Organs,* Job 21.11,12. Mr. *Caryls*[96] note on those words is, *That worldly men breed their Children vainly.* This is all their Religion. The Catechism which Wicked men teach their Children is to Dance and to Sing. Not that Dancing, or Musick, or Singing are in themselves sinful: but if the Dancing Master be wicked they are commonly abused to Lasciviousness, and that makes them to become abominable. But will you that are Professors of Religion have your Children to be thus taught? the Lord expects that you should give the Children who are Baptized into his Name another kind of Education, that you should bring them up in the nurture and admonition of the Lord: And do you not hear the Lord Expostulating the case with you, and saying, you have taken my Children, the Children that were given unto me; the Children that were solemnly engaged to renounce the Pomps of Satan; but is this a light matter that you have taken these my Children, and initiated them in the

96. Caryl, Joseph, (1602-1673), nonconformist leader and commentator.

{ 58 }

Pomps and Vanities of the Wicked one, contrary to your Covenant? What will you say in the day of the Lords pleading with you? we have that charity for you as to believe that you have erred through Ignorance, and not wickedly: and we have therefore accounted it our Duty to inform you in the Truth. If you resolve not on Reformation, you will be left inexcusable. However it shall be, we have now given our Testimony and delivered our own Souls. *Consider what we say, and the Lord will give you understanding in all things.*

F I N I S

A Cloud of Witnesses

First page of Cotton Mather's
A Cloud of Witnesses
Courtesy The Beinecke Rare Book and
Manuscript Library, Yale University

A Cloud of Witnesses;

Darting out Light upon a CASE, too Unseasonably made Seasonable to be Discoursed on.

THE CASE before us, is not, Whether People of Quality may not Employ a *Dancing-Master*, with due Circumstances of Modesty to instruct their Children how to carry themselves handsomely, in Company ? But, whether the *Dancing Humour*, as it now prevails, and especially in *Balls*, or in circumstances that Lead the Young People of both Sexes, unto great Liberties with one another, be not a *Vanity* forbidden by the Rules of Christianity ? And, If it be so, Whether Vertuous and Prudent Parents, will not by Second Thoughts be very cautious, how far expose their Children to the Temptations of such a *Vanity* ? If a *Nonconformist* Minister should speak to this CASE, it may be thought Answer enough, That it is HE. Wherefore that the Reader may have no pretence to be Angry at any One such Minister, in the World, we will only bring some other Authorities.

'Tis fit we should begin with, The Sacred Scripture.

Rom. XIII. 13.
Let us walk honestly, [or decently] *but not in*
RIOTING.

A   1 Pet.

Cotton Mather
Courtesy American Antiquarian Society

A Cloud of Witnesses;

Darting out Light upon a CASE, *too Unseasonably made Seasonable to be Discoursed on.*

THE CASE before us, is not, Whether People of Quality may not Employ a *Dancing-Master*, with due Circumstance of Modesty to instruct their Children how to carry themselves handsomely, in Company? But, whether the *Dancing Humour*, as it now prevails, and especially in *Balls*, or in circumstances that Lead the Young People of both Sexes, unto great Liberties with one another, be not a *Vanity* forbidden by the Rules of Christianity? And, If it be so, Whether Vertuous and Prudent Parents, will not their Second Thoughts be very cautious, how far they expose their Children to the Temptations of such *Vanity*? If a *Nonconformist* Minister should speak to this CASE, it may be thought Answer enough, That it is HE. Wherefore that the Reader may have no pretence to be Angry at any One such Minister, in the World, we will only bring some other Authorities.

'Tis fit we should begin with, The Sacred Scripture.

1. *See p.* 34 *of* Arrow.

Rom. XIII. 13.[1]

Let us walk honestly, [or decently] *but not in* RIOTING.

1 Pet. IV.2.

The Time past of our Life may suffice us, to have wrought the Will of the Gentiles,
2. *See p.* 34 *of* Arrow.
when we walked in REVELLINGS.[2]

All the World, that understand the Greek Tongue, (and the greatest Interperters) confess, That the Greek word, κωμος *Komos,* which our Translators, in one place render, by, RIOTING, in another, by, REVELLING, is truly translated, by DANCING. 'Tis the very Thing, Expresly forbidden.

The ASSEMBLIES Larger Catechism.

Q. *What are the Sins forbidden in the Seventh Commandment?*

A.—*Light Behaviour,—Unchast Company. —*

DANCINGS, *Stage-playes, and all other Provacations to Uncleanness in our selves or others.*

Behold, A great Authority, and REASON with it.

Phil. IV.8.

Whatsoever things are of GOOD REPORT,
3. *See p.* 36 *of* Arrow.
Think *on these things.*[3]

We will proceed unto some faithful Citations, from *Fathers,* yea, from *Pagans;* from *Councils:* from Divines of the Church of ENGLAND; yea, from *Roman-Catholicks,*

{ 66 }

and even *Courtiers* among them too: And
we will not Cite so much as one word from
any English *Nonconformists*, (who do not
use to declare for less Vertue, than the rest
of mankind!) that we may have some Account of the GOOD REPORT, which the
Thing before us has had among all the
Vertuous:

FATHERS.

The words of *Chrysostom*,[4] and of *Ar-*   4. *See p.* 40 *of* Arrow.
nobius,[5] and of *Austin*,[6] and other Ancient   5. *See p.* 40 *of* Arrow.
Writers, are so full of Terrors and Thunders,   6. *See p.* 40 *of* Arrow.
against the *Dances* of their Times, that ours
will not bear to hear them. We will be so
complaisant, unto the *Modern* Customes, as
only to Summ them up in this Epitome; *A*
Dance, is a Work of Satan, one of his Pomps
and Vanities, which all Baptised Persons
are under Vows to Renounce.

Only we will make so free with *Ambrose*,[7]   7. *See p.* 40 *of* Arrow.
(who was no *Non-Conformist*, but a *Bishop*,
and a *Courtier* too!) as to quote his Advice;
That if Godly Parents would not have the
Souls of their Children corrupted and
Ruined, they should be very cautious about
sending them to the Dancing School.

PAGANS.

Macrobius[8] informs us, That amongst An-   8. *See p.* 44 *of* Arrow.
cient Romans, *Dancing* was look'd upon as
Infamous.

Scipio Africanus,[9] complained of it, as a   9. *Ibid.*

{ 67 }

Degeneracy in his Age, that Persons of Quality sent their Children to the *Dancing School.*

10. See p. 44 of Arrow. *Salust,*[10] the Historian, reproached *Sempronia* as infamous, for having been a *Dancer;* their practice being, *The Instrument of Luxury.*

11. Ibid. *Cicero,*[11] in his Oration from *Muræna,* says, *Nemo Saltat Sobrius, nisi forte insaniat.* A man must be either *Drunk,* or *Mad,* (says the Orator,) that is fond of *Dancing.* He Says, *That this Vice never goes alone;* & therefore he Reproaches *Gabinius* & *Antonius* with it.

12. See p. 45 of Arrow. *Seneca*[12] bewails it, That in his Time Young ones were corrupted with *Dances;* and that *Dancing-Schools* were set up in the *13. Ibid.* City. *Tiberius*[13] himself, Banished the Dancers out of the City.

14. Ibid. *Priamus,*[14] in the Poet, severely reproves his Children, Because he understood they were, ορχησται *Dancers.*

15. Ibid. *Plutarch,*[15] in his Description of, *A Vertuous Woman,* mentions this, as part of her Character, *She must not be a Dancer.*

C O U N C I L S.

It is well known, That the old *Councils,* Ordained no less a Censure, Than that of *Deposition* for a *Clergy-Man,* and that of *Excommunication* for *other People,* to bear a part in a *Dance.* Particularly, One assembled in *Trullo*. Can. 51. Yea, very many Councils, make it a Crime in *Clergy-Men* to be so much as the *Spectators* of a *Dance*.

We will decend unto late ones.

Many provincial Assemblies in *Holland,* have declared, That the Scourge of *Ecclesiastical Discipline* should be employed upon *Dancers*.

The National Synod of *Dort*, A. 1578. thus Express themselves.

"Because Dances are for the most part attended with a levity, unbecoming Christians, and are an offence to the Godly; Especially when practised in a Time of Common Danger and Calamity: they that go to Dances shall be Reproved; and if after divers Admonitions they persist therein, they are to be excluded from communion."

The Reforming Synod in *Poland*, prohibited the *Dances* too commonly practised; and pronounced them censurable.

The Discipline of the Reformed Churches in *France*, has this Article.

"Dancing is to be suppressed; and those that take the Liberty or Custome to Dance, after they have been several times admonished, shall be Excommunicated, when they shew themselves obstinate in their Rebellion. And the consistories are Exhorted well to put this Article into Execution, and to Read the same Publickly in the

[Read this, *Ye Dancing Refugees,* and Reflect on Your Strange conduct under the dreadful Judgments of God]

{ 69 }

Name of God, and in the Authority of the Synods: And the said Synods and Colloquies are Exhorted to take heed of, and warn those Consistories that therein do not their Duties, to Censure the offenders for it.

And in this, 'tis well known, they did but imitate the old *Waldenses*.[16]

Divines of the Church of ENGLAND.

Three famous Bishops, have Written against *Mixt Dances*, as unlawful. Their *Names* are, Dr. *DOWNHAM*,[17] Dr. *BABINGTON*,[18] Dr. *ANDREWS*.[19] Their words are too long to be Repeated.

An Arch-Bishop, namely, Dr. *USHER*,[20] has Written against these Vanities, particularly in his Catechism. Page 279.

Yea, divers have more lately had the Courage to do so. Amongst the rest, Mr. H. *DeLuzancy*, the Vicar of *Harwich*. In his Treatise of the *Two Sacraments*, he showes, That *Baptised* Persons *are to Renounce the Pomps and Vanities of this sinful World*. And says he, p. 91,92 "Such are the Vain Conversations, Empty Visits, & Publick Meetings of People of Different Sexes, where the Soul is betray'd by the Eye, and Sinful Creatures are proud of poysoning one another. Such are those Methods of Dressing, which are grown a Study and a Trade; and Women are ashamed to appear with the Faces which God has given them, but

16. See p. 41 of Arrow.

17. See p. 43 of Arrow.

18. Ibid.

19. Ibid.

20. Ibid.

{ 70 }

choose rather to be seen with those of the Devils making. Washing, Painting, PATCHING, are become serious Occupations, and have turn'd out of Doors Morning Devotions. Such are BALLS, and Playes."

R O M A N - C A T H O L I C K S.

How can *Protestants* Expect any other, but that the Vengeance of Heaven, will Employ the *Papists* to Chastise them, to Destroy them, when *Protestants* indulge themselves in Vanties, which are decried and condemn'd even by the very *Papists?*

We know not what *Broad-sides* may quickly be given us, from *French Roman-Catholicks*. But there shall Two be now (instead of many more) turned upon us.

Father *Le Jeune*,[21] in his *Le Missionarie de L'Oratoire*, has a whole Sermon, *Contre Les Bals, Les Danses, et autres divertisemens mondains, qui sont allumettes de Luxure.*

21. Father Le Jeune (Jean Le Jeune 1592-1672) surname "Le Pere L'aveugle," a French orator. His Le Missionarie de L'Oratoire was printed in 1662 in 10 vol. "Balls and Dances" Vol. 2 - Sermon LXII.

I will faithfully Translate a few passages out of it.

"The Evil Spirit, has invented and introduced into the World, BALLS, and DANCES, and other Divertisements, which the *Reproved* call *Innocent,* but St. *Augustin* called, *Lugendas Latitias, The Sports which call for Sorrows.*"

He proceeds to show, how the Sacred Scriptures, which command *Seriousness,* and *Gravity,* and *Modesty,* condemn *Dances,* and begs his Hearers to think on that word; Job.21.11,13. *Their Children* DANCE, *and in a moment they go down to the Grave;* (or as he renders it,) *into Hell.* Says he; *There are some Sins thought Venail, that will End so.*

[*The men of* Rome, *shall rise in Judgment with this Generation, and shall condemn it!*]

He mentions and commends *Chrysostom,* who having heard, That some of his Hearers had been at a *Ball,* immediately he Preached a powerful Sermon against it; and among other things that man of God said, (& his words are quoted with Honour by this *Papist;*) *If I could Learn, who they were, that were present at these Follies, I would chase them out of the Church; I would not permit them to be present at our dreadful Mysteries;* And he goes on to call them, *The Pomps of the Devil.*

The Papist goes on to tell us, That *Chrysostom* observes, *We read not of any Dances at the Weddings of the Holy Patriarchs, and that the Weddings had the Blessings of God the more following of them.*

This Papist proceeds; 'When you were *Baptised,* you Renounced these *Follies;* you were Engaged by an Express promise, to shun these *Pomps of the Devil.* If you return to them, you are guilty of *Perfidy,* & *Forgery,* and *Disloyalty.* But how then can one

{ 72 }

grant you the *Communion* which is much more than *Baptism?'*

Says he; 'Here you throw away the precious *Time,* which cannot be recovered; the *Time* which is allowed you to work out your Salvation. You Extinguish in your selves the Spirit of *Piety,* of *Charity,* and of *Repentance;* the Spirit of *Devotion.* That Spirit is a precious Balm; or an Essence and a Cordial; nothing so easily grows Dead and Flat: there needs but *One Dissolute Hour,* to ruine in you, all that Spirit of Piety, which you have been gathering for many weeks, by your Meditations, and Supplications. They have no Speech of GOD, at a *Ball,* or at a *Play;* and if at *Collations,* they Speak of GOD, and of Divine Things, of Devotions or of Devout Persons, it is ordinarily to rally upon them, and tell merry Stories thereof.

'Here are profuse Expences of what should be Employ'd for the Comfort of the Poor, and their Succour in their Miseries.

'If the Young Gentlewomen would be well provided for in a Marriage, they should prefer a man of Sense and Judgement. Now there is no man of Judgement, who would not choose rather a Young Gentlewoman, that should be Wife, Modest, Reserv'd, and Retired, than a *Dancer,* a giddy, and an idle Damsel.

'Whence comes it that the *Casuist* informs me not, that the *Ball* and the *Play*, are any other than Indefferent Things? But think you to be Excused from the Judgements of God, because your Faith has been pinn'd on the Sleeve of, an *Alamode Casuist,* who has a mind to render himself complaisant unto your Inclinations, rather than harken to St. *Augustin,* and St. *Chrysostom,* and St. *Cyprian,* and other Fathers of the Church, who *Flatter* you not, because they *Need* you not.'

But, because this was a *Church-man,* we will hear no more from him. Let us at last hear a *Courtier.*

22. M. *Rabutin (Count de Bussy-Rabutin, Roger, 1618-1693), A celebrated French officer and writer.*

M. *Rabutin,*[22] in his Instructions to his Children. [In his *Memoirs,* Tom.2p.155.] has these passages. 'I have ever believed *Balls* to be dangerous. Of this, not only my *Reason,* but my own *Experience* made me sensible; and tho' the Authority of the *Fathers* of *the Church* in this Case, be very considerable, yet that of a *Courtier* may be of greater weight. The coldest Constitutions are inflamed there. They that are Old, cannot go to them, with out making a rediculous Figure, nor the Young, tho' within the Rules of Decency, without Exposing themselves to great Dangers. It is my Opinion, then, That A CHRISTIAN OUGHT NOT TO BE AT A BALL; and I think it the Duty of the *Guides* of *Consciences,* to Interdict it for ever unto those who are under their Direction.'

A *Question* upon the whole.

Whether a *Non-conformist Minister* can be justly Reproached, for his faithful and watchful Endeavours, to reclaim his Neighbours, from hazarding their own and their Childrens Vertue, by *Vanities,* which have had no *Good Report* by the Vertuous in all Ages, but been decired, not only by *Fathers,* by *Councils,* Divines of the Church of *England,* but also by *Papist,* both *Preachers* and *Courtiers,* and by the very *Pagans?*

Think seriously upon it; and upon Amos 6.3,5,6. *Wo to them that put far away the Evil Day, and chaunt to the sound of the Viol,—but they are not grieved for the Affliction of Joseph.*[23] And upon Isa. 22.12,13,14. *In that Day did the Lord God of Host call to weeping and to mourning; And behold Joy and Gladness; Surely, This Iniquity*[24]—*Look* it, Reader; for I Tremble to *Write it!*

23. See p. 48 of Arrow.

24. Isa. 22: 12,13,14 *And in that day did the Lord God of host call to weeping, and to mourning, and to baldness, and to girding with sackcloth: And behold joy and gladness, slaying oxen, and killing sheep, eating flesh, and drinking wine: let us eat and drink; for tomorrow we shall die. And it was revealed in mine ears by the Lord of host, Surely this iniquity shall not be purged from you till ye die, saith the Lord God of Hosts.*

A Bibliography of
Anti-Dance Books

Bibliography of Anti-Dance Books

PAUL MAGRIEL did a bibliography of dance tracts entitled, "Dancing and Morality." He also included anti-dance books in his *A Bibliography of Dancing*. However, his article for the *Bulletin of Bibliography* included mainly the books in the now defunct Dance Archives of the Museum of Modern Art in New York City.

The following bibliography is more complete and where possible the place where the book or tract can be found is listed. Those books that do not have a place listed were found in either an advertisement at the back of one of the books listed or in a dealer's catalogue of books.

The listing is as complete as possible but due to the nature of the material, it is always conceivable that a four page tract or sermon has been tucked out of sight. If so, the author would appreciate it being brought to his attention.

KEY TO ABBREVIATIONS

AAS	American Antiquarian Society
ABHS	The American Baptist Historical Society

BBM	*Bulletin of Bibliography,* May-Aug., 1942. Paul Magriel, "Dancing and Morality"
CBI	*Cumulative Book Index,* year of book follows.
CHI	Concordia Historical Society
COB	College of the Bible, Lexington, Kentucky
LC	Library of Congress
DCHS	Deciples of Christ Historical Society
MA	Joseph E. Marks III Collection
NYPL	The New York Public Library
NYPLDCF	The New York Public Library Dance Collection Clipping File
UK	University of Kentucky
UTS	Union Theological Seminary
U.Va.	University of Virginia
YUL	Yale University Library

Adams, R.A. *The Social Dance.* Kansas City, Ka. The Author, 1921. 32 pp. LC.

An Address, to the Congregational Church, in Sangerfield: Stating Grievances of a Number of the Members of Said Church. By One of the Aggrieved Brethren. Utica, N.Y., Printed for the author, 1807. ? p. AAS.

Anderson, H.O. *Should a Christian Dance?* Book Stall, 1928. CBI 1928.

Anderson, P. *An Answer to Certain Queries On the Subject of Dancing.* Richmond, C.H. Wynne, Printer, 1847. 104 pp. U. Va.

Andrews, C.W. *The Incompatibility of Theatre-Going and Dancing With Membership in the Christian Church. An Address to the Clergy of the Convocation of the Valley of Virginia, to the People of Their Respective Parishes.* Philadelphia, Leighton Publications, 1872. 31 pp. BBM.

Bailes, P.M. *Is the Dance Dangerous?* Grand Rapids, Zondervan, 1946. 24 pp. ABHS.

Baily, Thomas Jefferson. *The Modern Dance*. St. Louis, J.W. McIntyre, 1889. ABHS.

Baptist Sunday School Committee. *Modern Dance, Denounced*. [Texarkana, Ark.Tex., n.d.] 8 pp. ABHS.

Baten, Anderson Edith. *The Social Dance*. St. Louis, J.W. McIntyre, n.d. ABHS.

[Bates, William Henry.] *The Worldly Christians's Trinity: Cards, Theatre, Dance; by a Harassed Pastor*. Boston, Watchword and Truth, 1905. 53 pp. LC.

Beederwolf, William Edward. *The Christian and Amusements. Is Dancing Sinful? Is Card-Playing Wrong? Is Theatre-Going Harmful?* Chicago, Glad Tidings Publishing Co., 1909. 53 pp. LC.

Benton, Harry. *Seven Reasons Why I Do Not Dance*. Eugene, Oregon, Bible University Press. n.d. CBI 1928.

——. *The Public School Dance*. Eugene, Oregon, Evangel, n.d. 16 pp. DCHS.

Beryl, [pseud.] editor. *Immorality of Modern Dances*. New York, Everett & Francis Co., 1904. 124 pp. LC.

Bitting, Charles Carroll. *Modern Dancing*. Richmond, H.K. Ellyson Printer, 1858. 23 pp. ABHS.

Block, F.E. *Defense of F.E. Block* [*To the Session of the Central Presbyterian Church:*] Atlanta, n.p. 1878. 16 pp. UTS.

Bonham, James W. *The Temple of Pleasure; or, Seeing Life, by the Rev. J.W. Bonham. . . .* 2nd Ed., New York, T. Whittaker 1900. 147 pp. NYPL.

Borden, E.W. *Dancing and Piety. A Discourse Showing the Incompatibility of Dancing With Spiritual Religion*. East Saginaw, Mich., Daily Courier Steam Printing House, 1875. 19 pp. UTS.

Bowers, Mrs. J. Milton. [pseud?] *The Dance of Life, An Answer to the "Dance of Death" by Mrs. Dr. J. Milton Bowers*. San Francisco, San Francisco News Company, 1877. 132 pp. LC.

Brandt, J.L. *What About the Modern Dance?* Cincinnati, Standard Publishing Company, 1922. 15 pp. DCHS.

Bromley, Henry Walter. *A Sermon On Popular Amusements*. Wilmore, Ky., The Religious Book Supply Company. [c1914] 36 pp. LC.

Brooke, John T. *A Little Thing Great; or, the Dance and the Dancing School. Tested, in a Few Plain Sermons*. New York, Robert Carter & Bros., 1859. 116 pp. NYPL.

Brookes, James H. *May Christians Dance?* St. Louis, J.W. McIntyre, 1869. 143 pp. UK., CHI.; NYPL., LC., MA.

——. *The Modern Dance*. Chicago, The Church Press, 189-? 119 pp. NYPL., LC.

Brown, Henry. "The Dance," *The Impending Peril or Methodism and Amusements; A Compilation of Testimony, Rules, Speeches and Articles on the Amusement Question with an Argument in Review.* Cincinnati, Jennings and Pye, [c1904.] pp. 32-43 LC.

Bryant, Alfred. *Ought Christians to Dance? A Discourse Preached at Niles, December 14, 1854.* Chicago, Griggs & Co., 1855. 32 pp. BBM.

Buck, William Claus. *May Christians Dance, Attend Theatres, Circuses or Play Games, &c?* Nashville, Southwestern Publishing House. Graves, Marks & Co., 1857. 36 pp. ABHS

Callaway, T.W. *Should Christians Dance?* Chicago, The Bible Institute, n.d. 4 pp. NYPLDCF, MA.

Campbell, Robert Clifford. I. "The Road to Suicide: The Modern Dance," II. "Christ Crucified in the Home of His Friends," III. "The Dance of Death." *Modern Evils.* New York, Fleming H. Revell Co., [c1933] pp. 15-46 LC.

Candler, W.A. *Theatre-Going and Dancing.* n.p. Publishing House M.E. Church, South. n.d. CBI 1912.

Carrara, John. "The Modern Dance, History of the Modern Dance," *Enemies of Youth.* Grand Rapids, Zondervan, 1942. pp. 15-79 LC., CHI.

Cave, William Davis. *The Trio* [On Baptism, the Lord's Supper and Dancing.] [St. Louis,] J.W. McIntyre, n.d. ABHS.

Chappell, Clovis G. *The Modern Dance; Three Sermons.* Nashville, Publishing House M.E. Church, South, [c1923.] 48 pp. LC, NYPL.

Conant, Judson E. "The Dance." *Is the Devil in Modern Amusements?* Chicago, The Bible Institute Colportage Ass'n., [1936] pp. 14-20 NYPL.

Crane, J. Townley. *An Essay on Dancing.* New York, Carlton & Portor, 1849. 139 pp. LC., NYPL, MA.

——. "Dancing." *Popular Amusements.* Cincinnati, Hitchock & Walden, 1869. pp. 78-89 LC.

Crombie, Albert Harrison. "Is It Wrong to Dance?" *Rounds With the Devil; or Customs and Amusements.* Chicago, Glad Tidings Publishing Co., 1921. pp. 47-60 LC.

Culpepper, J.B. *Dance Shown Up.* n.p. Pentecostal Publishing Co., n.d. CBI 1928.

{ 82 }

Dallmann, William. *The Dance*. Pittsburgh, American Lutheran Publication Board, 1903. CHI.

Dance. n.p. Christian Witness Co. n.d. CBI 1928.

Dancing: Its Influence on the Character and Example of the Christian. Hartford, Edwin Hunt, 1847. NYPLDCF

Dancing: Social Dancing for the Purposes of Amusements–Is the Practice Consistent with the Christian Profession and Life? Philadelphia, A.B.P.S., n.d. 12 pp. ABHS.

Davis, C.A. *Dances and Dancing School*. Cumberland, n.p., n.d. CBI 1902.

Davis, George R. *Account of Trial of Social Dance*. New York, Rondout, 1899. 46 pp. LC, BBM.

Dexter, John H. *Waltzing...* Boston, n.p. 1868? 4 pp. BBM.

"Die Bibel und der Welt uebliche Tanz," Zwickau: Johannes Hermann, published by Deutsch, Amerikanischen Evang. - Luther. Traktat-Verein, 1894. CHI.

Dillon, John. *From Dance Hall to White Slavery*, New York, The Padell Book and Magazine Co., 1939. CHI.

Donaldson, Heber. *Dancing, Is it a Sin? Trial and Suspension of Heber Donaldson of Oil City, Pennsylvania.....* Oil City, Pa., Ormston & Hosey, 1881. 39 pp. LC.

Drumm, Melvin C. *The Modern Dance and What Shall Take Its Place*. [Center Hall, Pa., Center Reporter Printing Office, 1921.] 15 pp. LC.

Dye, William Milburn. "Dancing," *Popular Amusements and Their Substitutes*. Louisville, Ky., Pentecostal Publishing Co., 1912. pp. 9-29 LC.

E...Y...*Dancing as a Social Amusement, by Professed Christians, or Their Children*. New York, American Tract Society, [18--] 18 pp. NYPL, MA.

An Essay on Dancing, in a Series of Letters to a Lady Wherein the Inconsistence of that Amusement with the True Spirit of Christianity is Demonstrated. Philadelphia, n.p. 1825. 34 pp. NYPL.

Evans, W. Fairlie. *Theft and Promise of Life...* n.p. Christ Church [etc.] Presbyterian Bookroom. [1945?] 48 pp. NYPL.

Faulkner, Thomas A. *The Gates of Death; or the Ballroom Unmasked*. Los Angeles, Cal., T.A. Faulkner & Co. [1899] 94 pp. LC.

——. *The Gates of Hell; or, Eastern Ballroom Un-*

masked. Columbus, Ohio, Hussey & Faulkner, 1896. 94 pp. LC, NYPL.

——. *The Lure of the Dance.* Los Angeles, The Author, 1916. 148 pp. CHI, NYPL.

——. *From the Ballroom to Hell.* Chicago, The Henry Publishing Co., 1892. 72 pp. NYPL, LC, CHI, MA.

A *Few Reflections Upon the Fancy Ball, Otherwise Known as the City Dancing Assembly.* Philadelphia, C.R. Lilibridge, 1828. 16 pp. BBM.

Fife, Clyde Lee. "Amusements," *Fife's Revival Sermons.* Louisville, Pentecostal Publishing Co., 1922. pp. 191-226 COB.

Fowler, Philmon H. *Social Dancing As An Amusement for Professing Christians. A Discourse Delivered in the First Presbyterian Church.* Utica, N.Y., Roberts, Printer, 1859. 32 pp. NYPL.

Franklin, Benjamin. "Dancing," *The Gospel Preacher: A Book of 21 Sermons.* Cincinnati, G.W. Rice, 1878. 3rd Ed., Vol. II. pp. 385-409 COB.

From the Ballroom to the Grave. Rondleman, N.C., Pilgrim Tract Society, Inc., [19--] 4 pp. COB.

Gardner, William W. *Modern Dancing: In the Light of Scripture and Facts.* Louisville, Ky., Baptist Book Concern, 1893. 104 pp. LC, ABHS.

——. "Objection to Modern Dancing," *Missiles of Truth: With An Introductory Essay.* Louisville, A.C. Caperton & Co., 1883. pp. 290-304 UK.

Garnett, Mrs. F. *Dancing: Religion and Revelry.* Louisville, Ky., Ford & Robertson. 1858. 183 pp. ABHS

Guernsey, Jesse. *A Discourse on the Evils of the Dance, Delivered in the First Cong. Church, Derby, Conn. Dec. 22, 1850.* Birmingham, T.M. Newson, 1850. 16 pp. BBM.

Hall, George F. *Pitfalls of the Ballroom.* Chicago, Laird : Lee, 1901. 240 pp. NYPL.

Ham, Mordicai Fowler. *The Dance. Sermon Preached in Palestine, Texas, during Ham-Rumsey Meeting, May & June, 1914.* Palestine, Texas, Herald Print, n.d. 23 pp. ABHS.

——. *The Modern Dance; A Historical and Analytical Treatment of the Subject; Religious, Social, Hygiene, Industrial Aspects As Viewed by the Pulpit, the Press, Medical Authorities, Municipal Authorities, Social Workers, etc.* San Antonio, The San Antonio Printing Co., 1916. 60 pp. LC.

Harding, U.E. *After the Ball*. Grand Rapids, Mich., Zondervon, 1942. 57 pp. 1943. CBI.

Hart, Oliver. *Dancing Exploded. A Sermon Showing the Unlawfulness, Sinfulness, and Bad Consequences of Balls, Assemblies, and Dances in General; Delivered in Charleston, S.C., 1778*. Charleston, S.C. Printed by David Bruce, 1778. 32 pp. Evens 15848. NYHS.

Hawley, Bostwick. *Dancing as an Amusement, Considered in the Light of the Scripture of Christian Experience and of Good Taste*. N.Y., n.p. 1877.

Haydn, H.C. "The Dance," *Amusements, in the Light of Reason and Scripture*. N.Y., American Tract Society, [1880.] pp. 114-126 LC, NYPL.

Hecker, J.F.C. *Dancing Mania*. n.p. Humboldt, n.d. CBI 1902.

Heckman, George C. *Dancing As A Christian Amusement*. Philadelphia, Presbyterian Board of Publications, [c1879.] 36 pp. NYPL, LC.

Henderson, James A. "The Dancing Damsel," *Kentucky Conference Pulpit: Being Sermons by Ministers of the Kentucky Conference of the Methodist Episcopal Church, South, on Doctrinal, Practical, and Scientific Subjects. Compiled by the Rev. R. Hines, D.D.* Nashville, Publishing House of the Methodist Church, South, 1874. pp. 617-624 COB, UK.

Henkle, Moses M. "Amusements-Dancing," *Primary Platform of Methodism; or, Exposition of the General Rules*. Louisville, Ky., Morton & Griswold, 1851. 241-261 pp. LC.

Henry T. Charlton. "Dancing," *An Inquiry Into the Consistency of Popular Amusements With a Profession of Christianity*. Charleston, S.C., Wm. Riley, 1825. pp. 71-94 LC, NYPL, UTS.

Herman, William. [pseud.] *The Dance of Death*. San Francisco, H. Keller, 1877. 131 pp. NYPL, MA.

Hill, Sir Richard. *An Address to Persons of Fashion, Relating to Balls: With a Few Occasional Hints Concerning Play-Houses, Card-Tables, &c., In Which is Introduced the Character of Lucinda, A Lady of the Very Best Fashion and Most Extraordinary Piety. . . By a Member of the Church of England*. Boston, Printed by W. McAlpine, 1767. Evens 10644, 77 pp. LC, NYPL, CU.

Holt, B.M. *Is Dancing A Sin?* Fargo, N.D., n.p. 1920. CHI.

Hubbert, J.M. *Dancers and Dancing; A Calm and Rational View of the Dancing Question.* Nashville, Cumberland Presbyterian Publishing House, 1901. 44 pp. LC, UK.

Hughes, M.S. *Dancing and the Public Schools.* New York, Methodist Book Co., 1917. 29 pp. NYPL.

Hulot, Mathieu. *Balls and Dancing Parties Condemned by the Scriptures, Holy Fathers, Holy Councils, and Most Renowned Theologians of the Church. Advise to Young Persons Regarding Them.* Boston, P. Donahue, 1857. 216 pp. NYPL, UK, UVa.

Humphrey, Don. *What Makes Dancing Wrong.* Dallas, Christian Pub. Co. [c1963]. 37 pp. DCHS

Hunt, Marion Palmer. "Is there any harm in dancing?" A sermon preached in 22nd & Walnut St. 1894. Louisville, Printed by H.A. Kunnecke, n.d. 35 pp. ABHS

Ide, Jacob. *The Nature and Tendency of Balls, Seriously and Candidly Considered, in Two Sermons.* [Amherst, Mass., H. Davis, 1818?] 36 pp. NYPL, MA.

The Incompatibility of Theatre-Going and Dancing with Membership in the Christian Church. An Address of the Clergy of the Convocation of the Valley of Virginia, to the People of Their Respective Parishes. Philadelphia, Office of Leighton Publications, 1872. 31 pp. UTS.

Jackson, Rev. James C. *Dancing: Its Evils and its Benefits.* Dansville, N.Y., Austin, Jackson & Co., 1868. 23 pp. BBM.

Janes, D.C. *Dancing.* Louisville, Ky., Author n.d. 4 pp. DCHS.

Jones, John G. *An Appeal to All Christians, Especially the Members of the Methodist Church, Against the Practice of Social Dancing.* St. Louis, P.M. Pickard, 1867. 66 pp. LC.

Jones, Sam. "Dancing and Drinking," "The Round Dance," *Sam Jones' Anecdotes and Illustrations.* Chicago, Rhodes & McClure Publishing Co. 1898. p. 48 & pp. 231-232 COB.

Kerr, Robert Pollok. *The Dance, the Card Table, the Theatre, and the Wine Cup.* Richmond, Va., The Presbyterian Committee of Publications, [1898] 24 pp. LC.

Kirtzmann, P.E. *That Vexing Question.* St. Louis, Concordian Seminary Memograph Company, 1942. CHI.

Lamphear, Guy A. *The Modern Dance, a Fearless Discussion of a Social Menance.* Chicago, Glad Tidings Publishing Co., 1922. 64 pp. CHI.

Lewis, Franklin F. *Five Reasons Why Methodists Don't Dance.* Chicago, Glad Tidings Publishing Co., 1921. 71 pp. BBM.

Lindwall, C.A. *Dance.* n.p. Augustana, n.d. CBI 1928.

Lodge, James Llewellyn. *A Time To Dance.* New York, Ward & Drummond, [n.d.] 43 pp. ABHS.

Lowber, J.W. "Is It Wrong to Dance?" *The Devil in Modern Society.* Cincinnati, Standard Publishing Co. 1888. pp. 1-10 CHI, COB, DCHS.

Lyman, William. *Modern Refinement, or the Art of Dancing, as Taught and Practiced at the Present Day, Considered in Reference to its Moral Tendency.* New London, S. Green, 1801. 20 pp. NYPL, AAS.

Mather, Cotton. *A Cloud of Witnesses; Darting Out Light Upon a Case, too Unseasonably Made Seasonable to be Discoursed On.* Boston, Printed by [B. Green & J. Allen] [1700] 8 pp. YUL.

[Mather, Increase.] *An Arrow Against Profane and Promiscuous Dancing Drawn Out of the Quiver of the Scriptures by the Ministers of Christ at Boston in New England.* Boston, Samuel Green, 1685. 30 pp. Micro LC, NYPL.

Mathes, J.M. "The Time To Dance," *The Western Preacher.* St. Louis, Christian Publshing Co., 1888. pp. 475-480 COB.

Meade, Right Rev. William. *Baptismal Vows and Worldly Amusements.* New York, Protestant Episcopal Society for the Promotion of Evanglical Knowledge, [1850's?] pp. 30-40 COB.

Mesick, John S. *Discourse on the Evils of Dancing.* Harrisburg, Pa., Vestry, Theo. Fenn, Printer, 1846. NYPLDCF.

Meyer, Fulgence. *On Or Off With the Dance? A Familiar Talk On Dancing.* n.p. St. Francis Bookshop, n.d. 16 pp.

The Modern Dance. Randleman, N.C., Pilgrim Tract Society, Inc., C1955. 4 pp. COB.

The Modern Social Dance. St. Louis, J.W. McIntyre, n.d. ABHS.

Morey, Rev. A.B. *Dancing.* Cincinnati, Western Tract Society, n.d. 32 pp. MA.

Morris, Rev. Chamus Asbury. "Dancing," *Miscellany:*

Consisting of Essays, Biographical Sketches and Notes of Travel. Cincinnati, L. Swormslids & A. Pie, 1854. pp. 137-143 COB.

Morris, Melvin G. *The Devil's Ball; or, The Modern Dance.* Baltimore, Old-Time Religion Co., 1920. 52 pp. LC.

Neill, Edward Duffield. *Michal, or Fashionable Dancing an Undignified Amusement for Christians.* St. Paul, Combs, 1859. 18 pp. BBM.

Orr, William W. "Dancing," *The Christian and Amusements.* Chicago, Moody Press, 1960. pp. 99-110 LC.

Palmer, B.M. *Social Dancing Inconsistent with the Christian Profession and Baptismal Vows.* Columbia, S.C., 1849. LC, CHI.

Penn, W.E. *There is No Harm in Dancing.* St. Louis, L.E. Kline, 1884. 58 pp. LC.

Pentecost, G.F. *The Christian and the Ballroom, or, the Essential Evil of the Dance of Modern Fashionable Life.* Minneapolis, Johnson, Smith & Harrison, 1879. 15 pp. ABHS.

Pfefferkorn, G.J. *Ist Tanzen Sünde?* Cheppewa Falls, Wis., F.J. Pfefferkorn, 1901. 66 pp. LC.

Phillips, John. *Familiar Dialogues on Dancing, Between a Minister and a Dancer; Taken From Matter of Fact With an Appendix Containing Some Extracts From the Writings of Pious and Eminent Men Against the Entertainments of the Stage, and Other Vain Amusements.* New York, T. Kirk, 1798. 39 pp. Evens 34373, AAS, Micro LC.

Phipps, Lee Ralph. "The Modern Dance," *Popular Amusements — Destructive and Constructive.* Nashville, Cokesbury Press, 1925. pp. 47-62 MA.

Porter, John Williams. *Dancers of the Dance.* Louisville, Ky., Baptist Book Concern, [1922] 1921-24 Supp. CBI.

Progressive Democracy in Religion: or Rejoinder of "Cleucus" [pseud.] to "Scrulator" [pseud.] Schenectady, Riggs, 1848. 48 pp. BBM.

Rice, John R. *What's Wrong With the Dance?* Grand Rapids, Mich., Zondervan Publishing House, [n.d.] 44 pp. ABHS, MA

Rice, Nathan Lewis. *A Discourse on Dancing.* Cincinnati, Presbyterian Book Depository, 1847. 24 pp. LC.

Rogers, John. *A Discourse on Dancing.....* Cincinnati, The Author, [C1840.] 24 pp. UK.

"Rousing Revelations of the Modern Dance Brought to

Light," *Reprint from The Messenger of God.* n.p. Friendless Publishing House, n.d. 20 pp. BBM.

Saltator, [pseud.] *A Treatise on Dancing.* Boston, Press of the Commercial Gazette, 1802. 99 pp. BBM.

Samson, George Whitefield. *Idols of Fashion and Culture; or, Lusts Bowed to and Served Through Social Customs Fostered by Fashion, Veiled by Culture.* Boston, J.H. Earle, 1891. 261 pp. ABHS.

Sartori, Luigi. *Modern Dances.* Collegeville, Ind., St. Joseph's Printing Office, 1910. 72 pp. LC, NYPL.

Scrutator, [pseud.] *A Letter to "Clericus" in Reply to His Addressed to "The Synod of Albany, on the Subject of Dancing," Wherein is Discussed the Question "Was it Right in "Clericus" to Write and Publish Such A Letter."* . . . Albany, The Spectator Office, 1848. 23 pp. BBM.

Sinks, Perry Wayland. "Seven Indictments Against the Modern Dance." *Popular Amusements and the Christian Life.* Chicago, The Bible Institute Colportage Association, 1889. pp. 21-45 NYPL, LC, UTS.

Smith, Florence E. *Dancing.* n.p. Christian Witness n.d., CBI 1912.

Smith, J.J. *Thirty-Four Reasons Why Christians Should Not Dance.* n.p. Pentecostal Pub., n.d. CBI 1928.

Stocking, Collis A. *A Study of Dance Halls In Pittsburgh, Made Under the Auspices of the Pittsburgh Girl's Conference, 1925.* Pittsburgh, n.p. 1925. 47 pp. LC.

Stough, Henry Wellington, *Across the Deadline of Amusements.* Chicago, Fleming H. Revell Co. [1912.] 148 pp. LC.

Straton, John Roach. *The Dance of Death., Should Christians Indulge?* New York, Calvary Baptist Church, [1921?] 66 pp. CHI, UK.

——. *Fighting the Devil in Modern Babylon.* Boston, The Stratford Company, [1929.] 287 pp. LC.

Talmage, T. DeWitt. "The Wicked Dances" *Sin–A Series of Popular Discourses.* Chicago, Rhodes & McClure Publishing Co., 1897. pp. 272-282 COB.

——. "Dancing," *Social Dynamite; or the Wickedness of Modern Society.* St. Louis, Holloway & Co., 1888. pp. 224-234 COB, MA.

[Thacher, George H.] *A Letter to the Synod of Albany, on the Subject of Dancing. Ought the Synod Take Action On This Subject? . . . by Clericus.* Albany, J. Munsell, 1847. 30 pp. NYPL, LC.

Thomason, D.R. "Dancing," *Fashionable Amusements.*
New York, J. Leavitt, 1831. pp. 97-124 NYPL, LC.
Time to Dance; with Essay by C.P. n.p. Anstadt, n.d. CBI
1912.
Tuttle, Rev. Joseph F. *Shall I Dance?* Philadelphia, Pres-
byterian Publication Com., 18--? 20 pp. NYPL.
Verhaag, Rev. L.C. (comp.) *Word on Dancing.* n.p.
Diederich-Schaefer Co. n.d. CBI 1912.
Vernon, Rev. S.M. *Amusements in the Light of Reason,
History, and Revelation.* Cincinnati, Walden & Stowe,
1882. pp. 95-130 LC, UK.
Vincent, John Heyl. *Better Not; a Discussion of Certain
Social Customs.* New York, Funk & Wagnalls Company,
1888. 86 pp. NYPL. LC.
Vincent, Marvin R. *Amusement; a Force in Christian
Training. Four Discourses. . .* Troy, N.Y., W.H. Young,
1867. 140 pp. LC.
——. *Religion and Amusement an Essay.* Troy, N.Y., Wm.
H. Young, 1867. NYPL, LC.
Vom Bruch, Harry W. *The Modern Dance and Other
Amusements.* Long Beach, Calif., Glad Gospel Press,
n.d. 64 pp.
——. *The Carnival of Death or the Modern Dance.* Rev.
Ed., Findlay, Ohio, Fundamental Truth Publishers, n.d.
80 pp. MA.
Walther, K.F.W. *Tanz and Theaterbesuch.* n.p.
Lutherischer Concordic Verlag, 1885. CHI.
Warner, Anna B. "Dancing," *Tired Church Members.* New
York, Hurst & Co., 1889. pp. 38-51 LC.
Weigle, C.F. *Dance of Death.* n.p. Pentecostal Publishing
Co., n.d. CBI 1928.
Williams, Milan Bertrand. "The Dance," *Where Satan
Sows His Seed; Plain Talks on the Amusements of Mod-
ern Society.* Chicago, Fleming H. Revell Co., 1896. pp.
49-125 LC.
Wilkinson, William Cleaver. *The Dance of Modern Soci-
ety.* New York, Okley, Mason & Co., 1869. 77 pp. NYPL,
UTS, LC, CHI, ABHS, MA.
Wilson, Samuel R. *Dancing. A Discourse On the Fashion-
able Amusement of Dancing.* Cincinnati, Ben Franklin
Steam Printing Establishment, 1854. 31 pp. NYPL, UK.
Winecoff, Jesse. *A Discourse on Modern Dancing.* Gettys-
burg, Pa., H.C. Nerenstadt, 1850. CHI.
Woman's Christian Temperance Union. *Dancing in the
Public Schools.* n.p. W.C.T.U., n.d. CBI 1928.

Wood, Frederick P. *Questionable Amusements.* Grand Rapids, Zondervan Publishing House, [1937.] 46 pp. CBI 1933.

Young, M.N. *What Is Wrong With Dancing?* Lubbock, Texas, Broadway Church of Christ, 1951. 6 pp. folder DCHS.

Indexes

GENERAL INDEX

Abraham, 57
Alting, (Altingus) Johann H.,
    37, 43
Ambrose, St., 40, 67
Ames, William, 43
Andrews, Lancelot, 43, 70
Antonius, 45, 68
Apes, 38
Arebella, 3
Aretius, Benedictus, 34, 42
Arnobius, 40, 67
*An Arrow Against Profane
    and Promiscuous* ..., 1,
    5, 7, 9, 15, 18, 19, 22-24
Assembly (Church), 32, 66,
    69
    Provincial, 56
Atheists, 38, 44
Augustin, St., 71, 74
Austin, (St. Augustine), 40, 67
Azorius, (Azor) Jean, 39

Babington, Gervase, 43, 70
Bacchus, 37
Beard, Thomas, 50
Bedlams, 36
Bishop, (Church), 43, 67
Bolton, Robert, 43
Boston, (England), 8
Boston Latin Grammar School,
    18
Boston, Massachusetts, 1, 2,
    4-7, 11, 12, 17, 22, 49
Bourree, 12
Bradford, John, 9
Brinsley, John, 43
Brownell, George, 17
Brunning, Joseph, 1, 22

Cajitan, Thomas Devio, 39
Caligula, 38
Calvin, John, 42
Cambridge, Massachusetts, 10

Caryl, Joseph, 58
Casuist, 39, 74
Catechism, 32;
    Larger, 32, 66;
    Dr. Usher's, 70
Cato, 45
Charles II, 2
Charlestown, Massachusetts, 9
Cheever, Exekiel, 18
Christ, 34
Christians, 35, 36, 38, 51
Chrysoston, St. John, 40, 67,
    72, 74
Church of England, 66, 70, 75
The Church of the Ungodly, 55
Cicero, 44, 68
A Cloud of Witnessess, (Cotton
    Mather), 17, 19, 20, 22-24
Colman, Benjamin, 2
Commandments, 42;
    Second, 6, 54;
    Seventh, 6, 9, 32, 33, 42, 66
Constaninople, 40
Contre Les Bals, Les Dance,
    (LeJune), 71
Councils, (church), 66, 68, 75
Country dance, 12
Courtier, 67, 74, 75
Cotton, John, 1, 8, 49
Cyprian, St., 74

Danaeus, (Daneau), Lambert,
    42
David, 51
DeLuzancy, H., 70
Devil, 3, 7, 39-41, 46, 50-52, 72
Diana, (goddess), 38
Dinah, 49-50
Dod, John, 43
Dorchester, Massachusetts, 1
Dort, 56, 69
Downham, John, 43, 70
Dublin, 1

INDEX OF BIBLICAL QUOTATIONS

ACKNOWLEDGEMENTS

I would like to thank The New York Public Library for permission to use its copy of the *Arrow*, the Yale University Library for permission to use *A Cloud of Witness*, and the many libraries and librarians who have given their time and help. The portraits of Cotton and Increase Mather are used by courtesy of the American Antiquarian Society.

I especially want to thank Dr. Merton England for his helpful suggestion as well as Mr. and Mrs. Charles Harber; also Martha Shindlebower who typed the manuscript.